Finding
the
Narrow Road

A Devotional Journey of My life

Williams family

Above everything on this
earth follow God, Jesus Christ,
and the Holy Spirit.
Join me in heaven.
Follow me as I follow Christ.
Psalms 118:8

Brenda Knox

Brenda Knox

ISBN 978-1-64515-024-4 (paperback)
ISBN 978-1-64515-025-1 (digital)

Copyright © 2019 by Brenda Knox

All rights reserved. No part of this publication may be reproduced, distributed, or transmitted in any form or by any means, including photocopying, recording, or other electronic or mechanical methods without the prior written permission of the publisher. For permission requests, solicit the publisher via the address below.

Christian Faith Publishing, Inc.
832 Park Avenue
Meadville, PA 16335
www.christianfaithpublishing.com

The Holman Christian Standard Bible (HCSB) translation used unless otherwise noted.

Printed in the United States of America

Reviews

Brenda Knox has written a 50 day devotional to enlighten and encourage others to choose the narrow road. She shares her vulnerabilities from life's tragedies and triumphs in an effort to glorify God in the process. Brenda shares her life story with truth and love and shows us how to choose God in all things along the way. Be encouraged by her testimony of faith and understand the way God pours out His grace and mercy as we travel the narrow road!

-Diane

Finding the Narrow Road presents a collection of personal stories and spiritual insights from Author Brenda Knox. Each vignette transports you, sometimes jolts you, to a specific memory throughout the warp and weft of Knox's life. Though jarring at times; the effect is remarkably real to life. Sometimes joyful, sometimes painful, Finding the Narrow Road is a story full of comedy, tragedy, and redemption, unflinchingly written and woven together by scripture.

-Renea

Warning

This is a book about my real life. Some stories will be hard to read. It is not a sugarcoated story. It is really what happened. It is about God's forgiveness and *love*, of how He helps those who make ignorant mistakes but still try to follow with all their heart, of how He brings us back to Himself.

The parts that are outlined are my true life story.

Acknowledgments

Thank you to my children, Henry, Thadeus, and Josiah, for being with me. Thank you to my friends, Venus, Laura, Chris, Wendy, Patty, Susan, and Jo Carol.

All of you believed in me. You didn't give up on me. I so appreciate the prayers you sent up to God for me. I can't thank all of you enough for your support.

Thank you, Jesus, for writing this book through me.

Day 1

The Beginning

Everyone who is alive has a story. Every story is as unique as our thumbprint. This is mine. My life started like most. I was born in a hospital in December of 1968. My mother told me about it. She went into labor later in the day. I was her sixth child. Since Dad was at work, she took the other five to a neighbor. When she arrived at the hospital, she almost had me in the elevator. I was almost dropped on my head. God protected me. We were in New Mexico at this time, then moved shortly after. Later I found out that we moved because my father was embarrassed by my mother. You may ask, how did she embarrass him? In the sixties, it was very frowned upon for anyone to commit adultery. Well, my mother also has Asperger syndrome. They didn't know what this was in the sixties. My dad knew something wasn't right in her thinking. My mom has no inhibition to just say whatever happens to come to her mind. She would go places and just talk about whatever she was doing and whoever she was doing it with. Not long after I was born is when we moved. I was then told we went to Texas, then Colorado, then quickly to Wyoming.

Thumbprint

Every person's life is unique. God is weaving the tapestry. He already knows His plan for our life. Even the things we perceive as bad are actually for our growth. Some of the things we endure are not about us at all. God has a perfect plan for everyone, plans to give us a future and a hope.

> For I know the plans I have for you this is the Lord's declaration—plans for your welfare, not for disaster, to give you a future and a hope. (Jeremiah 29:11)

Day 2

Young Memories

I remember Wyoming. We lived in two places there. I remember the snow and being sick. I was told it was chicken pox. Five of us had the chicken pox. Our oldest brother didn't get it. He thought that was funny. We had been inside for days. Mom didn't want to let us go out and play in the snow. Dad said, "Let them go. They are not going to get sicker than they have been."

I also remember a boy my age. He always repeated the word *mines*. He had a tricycle and rode around saying that word over and over. If you had a toy, he would look at it and say. "Mines."

I would be like, "No, this is mine not yours." One day my family was teasing me about him liking me. I was only two or three years old. I remember thinking I can't stand him always saying *mines*. There were other children that were older and played with my siblings. I was too young to know them. I was either four or five when we moved to Alabama.

Road Begins at Birth

There are two roads. One leads to heaven. One leads to hell.

> Enter through the narrow gate. For the gate is wide and the road is broad that leads to destruction, and there are many who go through it. How narrow is the gate and difficult the road that leads to life, and few find it. (Matthew 7:13–14)

I will use the road concept throughout this book. The road leading to hell is wide, and many are on it. For the most part, this road is easy and smooth to drive on. The road leading to *heaven* is small, and few find it. This road has many obstacles, potholes, and things will fly in your way. There will be times you get blindsided by something. Satan is trying to keep us from either finding the narrow road or knock us off it.

When we are born, we start life on the wide road. Our car may be being pulled behind our parents' car. Regardless of how or where your story began, soon we are detached to drive our car through our journey. This is when we start to make our decision on which road we want to be on.

Wide and Narrow

Satan is a liar. He is doing his best to deceive everyone. If you are on the wide road, then he already has you. If you switch to the narrow road, then the lies get more intense. On the wide road, Satan makes it easy and smooth so that you don't want to leave it. If you switch to the narrow road, Satan starts to attack, throwing obstacles in your way, making it hard to be on. That is when you need to be trusting fully in God.

> Therefore, when many of His disciples heard this, they said, "This teaching is hard! Who can accept it?" (John 6:60)
>
> Instruct them to do what is good, to be rich in good works, to be generous, willing to share, storing up for themselves a good reserve for the age to come, so that they may take hold of life that is real. (1 Timothy 6:18–19:18)
>
> Therefore, I say this and testify in the Lord: You should no longer walk as the Gentiles walk, in the futility of their thoughts. They are darkened in their understanding, excluded from the life of God, because of the ignorance that is in them and because of the hardness of their hearts. They became callous and gave themselves over to promiscuity for the practice of every kind of impurity with a desire for more and more. (Ephesians 4:17–19)

DAY 3

Church Beginnings

We moved to Alabama. I was very young, so my memories are in chunks. Alabama is where I first remember being told about God, Jesus Christ, and the Holy Spirit. I was the sixth child. Our mother sent us to church to get a break. The problem with that is it didn't matter which church, whoever would pick us up. I was too young to really understand anything that they were talking about. Also, the things we learned were not reinforced at home. We were only going because Mom made us go. It was just a part of my day. I didn't mind going, but I don't think the others liked it much.

Animal Love

Me and my two sisters went to the mail box to get the mail, and we found a possum had been killed. Then we noticed a baby was still alive. Babies whether humans or animals are so cute. It was sad to me that it had lost its mom. We took it home and tried to save it. It only lived a few more days. When I think back on this,

> I am grateful to my mom. This showed me a compassion for wildlife.
>
> We also used to play in the woods a lot. Once when we were in the woods, we saw a long black snake. We all lined up. We were not wanting to get bit by it. I was the youngest and very small, so I was in the back of the line. I was a little scared of snakes. I knew that some were poisonous. I think all of us had a little bit of what I call a healthy fear of the possible dangers of wildlife. We thought it might be dead because it was so still. My oldest brother tapped it with a stick. It went super fast away. Later we found out it was a black racer.

We Are Human Sheep

God cares for humans and animals. I believe that God wants us to love and care for all people and animals. Yes, some animals are to be for food. That does not mean you should be cruel to them. God calls us sheep.

> Because My flock has become prey and food for every wild animal since they lack a shepherd, for My shepherds do not search for My flock, and because the shepherds feed themselves rather than My flock. (Ezekiel 34:8)

We need to be about the business of finding and discipling those who will come to Christ. We are worth more than the animals.

> So don't be afraid therefore; you are worth more than many sparrows. (Matthew 10:31)

Day 4

Fun Times

Life is about all things. Some are just fun and funny.

On one afternoon, I went for a walk, and my second oldest brother was digging a rectangular hole in the sand. He asked me if I would cover him up to his neck when he got the hole finished. I said sure. When he got done, he laid down, and we both put the sand on him. I finished it and pat the sand down. He looked funny with just his head sticking out. We both laughed.

When we lived here, we would eat watermelon outside while we sat on the swing set and spit the seeds on the ground. This was really fun. We would get all sticky. Later we saw vines trying to grow around the swing set.

I remember I was playing outside near the road by myself. I don't know why I was there. All of a sudden, it started raining, just buckets of rain. I was drenched in a few seconds. I thought, *Well, I am already wet. I may as well play in it on the way home.* So I went stomping in the ditch beside the road. I had a lot of fun. I stepped in the front door. Everyone turned to look at me. I said as I dripped on the floor, "I got caught in the rain." They all laughed.

God Loves Laughter

Sometimes you just need to have fun and play. God doesn't want us to be prunes. I am sure that God laughs at us a lot. How appealing is a church full of prunes? I believe we are to have fun and enjoy life. In that process, we can reach the lost. Be a minister who is pleasant.

> Our mouths were filled with laughter then, and our tongues with shouts of joy. Then they said among the nations, the Lord has done great things for them. (Psalms 126:2)
>
> Strength and honor are her clothing, and she can laugh at the time to come. (Proverbs 31:25)
>
> A time to weep and a time to laugh; a time to mourn and a time to dance. (Ecclesiastes 3:4)

God knows and even has told us that this life will be troublesome. But He also wants us to trust Him and smile.

Day 5

Too Young to Know Better

This is also the first place I experienced smoking. I caught my oldest brother smoking on the back porch. He made me join him. He thought this would keep me from telling. However, he forgot how young I was. So when Dad asked who was smoking on the back porch. I innocently said me and my oldest brother. He got in trouble because I didn't know it was not okay. My brother got mad at me. I didn't understand why he was angry.

One day, we were all playing outside. My oldest brother thought it would be funny to put a ball in ants and pass it to me. I was running, and the others all started to scream at the same time. I couldn't understand what any of them were saying. When I started to feel ant bites, I knew then. I ran in the house crying. I told my parents as I ran to the shower. This was the first really mean thing I remember him doing. This really made me angry. I was also mad with my parents. I felt that my brother should've been punished. I really don't know what they did to him, if anything.

We moved down the road into a trailer park. We became friends with a family that lived across the highway from the trailer park. In the trailer park, one of the families had a little girl that I became friends with. I was only about five; she was only about three. One day we were all talking beside the highway at the front of the trailer park, the family from across the highway, the family with the little girl and us. We were the youngest ones there. The little girl had a new puppy. The puppy ran into the highway. There was a vehicle coming from both directions. No one was doing anything, but the girl was crying and very sad. It broke my heart. I couldn't stand that she might see her puppy killed. I ran in the road and picked up the puppy. I held him tight to me right in the middle of the road on the yellow line. One vehicle slowed down and went around. One vehicle had an older lady. She screeched to a stop and started yelling at me. Everyone was yelling at me. When I knew the danger was gone, I walked to the little girl. I pet the puppy and handed it to her. I had to ask one of my sisters about what I did next, because I went into a bit of shock and had forgotten. She said after I handed the puppy to her, I just walked away and went to my bed in our house. My mom came and asked how I was. That is when I cried, then the shock was over.

By now, we are all in school. We lived here a few years, then moved to another town in Alabama.

Young Christian

God wants us to be innocent children and tell Him everything. Sometimes as young Christians, we make terrible mistakes. We may run into danger and not even know that we are. God will help us, but He also wants us to grow and learn, building our faith and becoming strong.

So the church throughout all Judea, Galilee, and Samaria had peace, being built up and walking in the fear of the Lord and in the encouragement of the Holy Spirit, and it increased in numbers. (Acts 9:31)

The whole building, being put together by Him, grows into a holy sanctuary in the Lord. (Ephesians 2:21)

DAY 6

Divided House

> Back to the road. At this point, I am still on the wide road. We are being sent to churches, but I don't recall really being taught. At the age of six, I'm still traveling the wide road. Satan is happy when we don't find the narrow road or when we get off it. What I didn't know was that our house was divided. My mother was always going out. She would get other guys and have one-night stands. My father was on the narrow road, and my mother was on the wide road. If both parents are on the narrow road, we might find it sooner. If both are on the wide road, it will prove more difficult to find. When the parents are divided in their hearts, the children will have no direction. A house divided cannot stand.

Knowing their thoughts, He told them: "Every kingdom divided against itself is headed for destruction, and no city or house divided against itself will stand. If Satan drives out Satan, he is divided against himself. How then will his kingdom stand?" (Matthew 12:25–26)

If a house is divided against itself, that house cannot stand. And if Satan rebels against himself and is divided, he cannot stand but is finished! (Mark 3:25–26)

Knowing their thoughts, He told them: "Every kingdom divided against itself is headed for destruction, and a house divided against itself falls." (Luke 11:17)

Cloudy Thinking

> We have moved to another town in Alabama. The memories here are also in parts. When I was young, I was one of those kids you would say has their head in the clouds. Life was moving around me, and I wasn't paying much attention. This was actually good for me, as it protected me from many evil schemes. I didn't notice many of them, so attacks from the evil one bounced off. When I was directly attacked is when my awareness began.

Mind of Christ

Get your thinking clear, be sober in your thoughts. Know and learn who God, Jesus Christ, and the Holy Spirit are. Study the power in Jesus's name. If your mind is set on the things of this earth, it is not on Jesus and heaven. This earth and the things in it are fleshly.

> For the mind-set of the flesh is death, but the mind-set of the Spirit is life and peace. For the mind-set of the flesh is hostile to God because it does not submit

itself to God's law, for it is unable to do so. (Romans 8:6–7)

For who has known the mind of the Lord? Or who has been His counselor. (Romans 11:34)

Day 7

Children's Games

> We made the best of being poor. With so many children, most of your money goes to food and shelter. So we made up many games. One such game we could only do after a heavy rain. The backyard would flood, and this would bring up crawdads. We made up a game to see who could catch the most. I thought this was really fun. Maybe more fun because it had to rain first. I don't know what the others thought. We all seemed to have fun.
>
> ### Family Visits
>
> At times our uncle and aunt would come for visits. This was Mom's brother. Mom's parents also came for visits; these were really nice times. I remember Grandma always talking. She would just talk and talk. I liked seeing them. It was always a happy house while they were there.

Family Blessing

Because we are flawed humans, unfortunately some families are not blessings. Families are supposed to be there for each other to love and support one another. God loves the family unit. His desire is to bless the family. This is why we need to pray together. As Christians, we certainly should love one another in Christ.

> Show family affection to one another with brotherly love. Outdo one another in showing honor. (Romans 12:10)
>
> From whom every family in heaven and on earth is named. (Ephesians 3:15)
>
> You are the sons of the prophets and of the covenant that God made with your ancestors, saying to Abraham, and all the families of the earth will be blessed through your off spring. (Acts 3:25)

DAY 8

The Split

As I had said before, our house was divided. One night, I woke up to yelling. My parents were fighting hard. I looked out and saw my dad slap my mom. This is the only time I ever saw him hurt her. It was very soon after that they divorced. I learned much later that my mom had told him she loved someone else. My dad was a good man. The person my mother thought she loved got back with his wife. My dad let mom sleep in the bed and he slept on the couch until she found someone else.

For my father and mother, the divorce was simple. Mom did not work. So Dad kept us kids, and she remarried. People ask me, "How did you feel about your mom leaving?" It is sad to say. The only difference I remember is we had to start doing the housework. I didn't have much of a relationship with my mom. So I didn't really feel anything.

Naughty Boys

My older brothers started sneaking cigarettes from our dad. So we wouldn't tell they made the rest of us smoke.

I was actually inhaling the smoke. I got one of dad's non-filtered cigarettes, and I thought that I was not going to wake up the next day. I really thought I was going to die. I am sure I turned shades of green. When I did wake up the next day, I told them, "If you want to destroy your body go ahead." I never smoked again. This was more protection from God.

My oldest brother used to just randomly hit me real hard for no reason. Later in life, he said it was to make me tough. I think I was what he used to take his anger out on. On one Saturday morning, I did give him a reason to be upset. He took it too far. I was awake early. The dog was barking at something. I was telling the dog to stop. It has been said of me that I learned how to talk in a barn. For those who do not understand, it means I'm loud and don't need a microphone. Well, my brother who had been partying the night before was not happy about my loudness with the dog. He grabbed a little orange tube and came out and started hitting me with it. He hit me so hard he put welts on my arm. I still have the scars today. This hurt me more than just physically. When I look at the scars on my arm, it is a constant reminder. I have forgiven him, but forgetting won't happen.

Division

We must stand united. As families and as Christians, we are supposed to stand firm on the word of God. We can pray division in the enemies' camp. However, we need to stay in one accord. If someone promotes something that is not of

God, they need to be corrected. This way, we will be able to stand in the last days.

> But you, dear friends, remember what was predicted by the apostles of our Lord Jesus Christ; they told you, "In the end time there will be scoffers walking according to their own ungodly desires." These people create divisions and are unbelievers, not having the Spirit. But you, dear friends, as you build yourselves up in your most holy faith and pray in the Holy Spirit. Keep yourselves in the love of God, expecting the mercy of our Lord Jesus Christ for eternal life. (Jude 1:17–21)

Day 9

Special Christmas

> On one, Christmas our father made a very special gift. He built us all a wooden box. He put our initials on the top. This for me was such a special gift. I really love that box. I still have mine to this day.

Dad's Love

> Our dad had a welder. One day one of my brothers was using it. The sparks flew everywhere. Well, this started a fire in the shed. My brother called the fire department. They came and put it out. It had gotten into the trailer a little. Every tool my dad owned was gone. I was very nervous and scared at what he would do when he got home. I did not need to worry. I watched him closely. He had to walk down the driveway, because of all the cars. He looked around, and I saw his lips. One, two, three, four, five, six. He was counting his children. When he saw we were all okay, he went in the house and let the fire department finish their job. I was shocked. I went in the house to talk to him. I asked him if he was mad at us. He said, "No, there is nothing you can do about

> what happened. The right thing to do was call for help." He taught me many things by his actions that day. I don't do knee-jerk reactions like most. When bad things happen, I don't jump around with worry. My dad being calm that day has made me a much calmer person when things go crazy.

Too Short

> My brothers like to build bicycles. Back then, bikes were a little different. My legs are short. I could not reach the pedals. I was so upset. I went in the house and told my father I am not going to ride a bike again. He asked why. I said, "Because I have to wreck it to get off." A week later, he had ordered a tricycle and told the others they were not allowed on it. "This is for Brenda only." I had not even asked for it. I was so happy. I rode that tricycle all over every day. I rode it until the wheels came off. Finally I grew taller. What a blessing he had done for me.

Father's Love

As I live and learn, it is a little surprising how important a father's love is for children. I dare say in most people even more than the mother. There is something special when you hear your daddy say, "I am so proud of you." Our heavenly father is saying that to all of us Christians. When we serve Him faithfully, He is so proud of us. God loves you. You can trust Him.

> Even if my father and mother abandon me, the Lord cares for me. (Psalms 27:10)

God in His holy dwelling is a father of the fatherless and a champion of widows. (Psalms 68:5)

I will not leave you as orphans; I am coming to you. (John 14:18)

Day 10

Big Bite

On one occasion, I walked to the store by myself. Our dog had figured out that if he stood on the mat outside of the store, the door would open. So he would go inside and find us. On this day, we locked him up so he wouldn't follow me. I deeply regret this now. As I walked to the store, this black guy was on a brown bike, and he was watching me. This made me feel very uncomfortable. He was creepy. He had a cast past his ankle on one foot. He went away, so I thought, *I'm glad he left.* I was still very uncomfortable. I got to the store and made my purchase. I looked over the road before leaving the store. I didn't see that guy or anyone. I thought it looks safe. One my way back from the store, he popped up from nowhere and jumped me. He pulled me off to the side of the road. He was saying some nasty things to me as he was trying to take off my clothes. I could hear cars passing by. I think we were too low down for them to see us. He was trying to rape me. I was a biter. If my brothers or sisters were doing things to me, I would bite them. Out of instinct, I bit the guy's hand so hard I am sure I made him bleed. This is how I got away. I told my family what had happened, but at the same time, I didn't understand

what he was trying to do. This is how God protected me.
I think I was about eight when this happened. When I
was eleven, my family was watching a program. On this
program, a child got raped. I looked at my sister and said
that is what that guy was trying to do. She said, "Yeah, I
know. Didn't you know that?"
I said, "Not until now."

Face Plant

One day, my brother and sister wanted to go to the park. We rode our bikes. I had gotten a little taller and could finally reach the pedals. We played in the park for a while. The park was down a small hill. The hill was the driveway into the entrance. We decided to ride our bikes fast down the hill. Well, the bike I was on messed up. The pedals locked all of a sudden. I was going at such a high speed, I had a death grip on the handlebars. When the pedals stopped, I was unable to release the handlebars fast enough, and I flew over. My face landed teeth first on the asphalt. One of my front teeth broke in half. This could have broken my neck. I believe God protected me from that. However, damage was done to my neck and body.

Real Pain

We all have times in our lives with real pain. Some have more than others. Some of our pain is caused by others. Some is caused by ourselves. However we experience pain, it does not please God for us to hurt or to be hurt at the hands of others. Jesus understands all and any kind of pain we might have endured. When Jesus was put on the cross he had been so beaten, He barely looked like a human. Jesus can be trusted with your pain.

> See My servant will act wisely; He will be raised and lifted up and greatly exalted. Just as many were appalled at You His appearance was so disfigured that He did not look like a man, and His form did not resemble a human being so He will sprinkle many nations. Kings will shut their mouths because of Him, for they will see what had not been told them, and they will understand what they had not heard. (Isaiah 52:13–15)

Day 11

Who's Lying

> If any of you have multiple children, then you know it is hard to find out who did something. Well, I would not lie to my father or really anyone. Because I kept tattletaling on my brothers and my sisters, my brother decided (with the others in agreement) that they would all say I did everything from then on. Our father started to think that I was a liar. This hurt me real bad. I knew our dad didn't know the truth. I was very angry with my brothers and sisters. When I stopped the tattletale, they continued to lie about me. I don't remember them ever stopping this.

When We Lie

Lying does no one any good. Satan is the author of lies. Lying is a sin. Some people think that it is okay to lie if someone might get their feelings hurt. I would rather tell them a dress doesn't look good on them than let them wear it in public thinking that it is pretty on them only to have them find out later from someone else that it looks bad.

> You must not steal. You must not act deceptively or lie to one another. (Leviticus 19:11)

> Do not lie to one another, since you have put off the old self with its practices. (Colossians 3:9)
>
> I have not written to you because you don't know the truth, but because you do know it, and because no lie comes from the truth. Who is the liar, if not the one who denies that Jesus is the Messiah? This one is the antichrist: the one who denies the Father and the Son. (1 John 2:21–22)

Day 12

Mean Kids

> I did not like school. Mostly because of the other kids. Many were just plain mean. On one such occasion, I was walking to get to my bus. Kids on another bus that I didn't even know started yelling out, "You're ugly." This was just plain hateful even when you know that there is nothing true to what they are saying. You think, *Am I ugly? Am I really this or that?* Things like this, the devil uses to keep you from the narrow road. The words others say keep us feeling like God doesn't love us because _____ (you can fill in the blank). We need to be careful of the words we use. We should speak life to those around us.

What You Speak Matters

When we say hurtful things even if it was meant as a joke, it hurts deep. The devil also listens to the things we say. If we call someone lazy, he will attack them and has a right to attack them with a lazy demon. Tell people they are strong, that they have worth. Tell them they are loved. God loves everyone.

> A man is worth far more than a sheep, so it is lawful to do what is good on the Sabbath. (Matthew 12:12)

Consider the ravens: they don't sow or reap; they don't have a storeroom or a barn; yet God feeds them. Aren't you worth much more than the birds? (Luke 12:24)

For I consider that the sufferings of this present time are not worth comparing with the glory that is going to be revealed to us. (Romans 8:18)

Day 13

Nice Old Lady

> We used to play with the other kids in the area. One time, I was going to another kid's house to play. I saw an old lady on her porch. She waved at me. So I went over and sat on her porch and just talked. She was such a nice lady. I would go back to her house from time to time. Once I was telling her about a project the teacher had given us. We had to get the biggest leaf we could find, then tell about it. She said, "I have a big leaf for you." She cut an elephant ear leaf. It was almost bigger than me. I was so happy to have the biggest leaf of the class. She was such a nice lady. I loved to go and sit with her. She was so kind. She spoke love by her actions.

Love the Children

No matter if you have children or not, everyone should take time to be sweet to the children that live close. You have no idea what they are dealing with at home. Some children need kindness and a smile because they aren't getting it where they should be at their home.

> Jesus, however, invited them: "Let the little children come to Me, and don't

stop them, because the kingdom of God belongs to such as these. I assure you: Whoever does not welcome the kingdom of God like a little child will never enter it." (Luke 18:16–17)

I have no greater joy than this: to hear that my children are walking in the truth. (3 John 1:4)

Therefore, be imitators of God, as dearly loved children. (Ephesians 5:1)

Day 14

Heavenly Animals

> We kids were always finding stray dogs and cats. Our dad never complained about us bringing them home. We always had animals around. One of the dogs died, and a few weeks later, a cat died. When the dog died that night, I saw its spirit in the window. After the cat died, I saw it in the window also. I would have thought that I was just seeing things if my sister had not told me she saw it also. When I first saw the dog, I was a little freaked out. When I saw the cat, I think I waved good-bye. The next time our animals died, I watched the window, but I didn't see anything ever again. Does this mean our pets go to heaven? I don't know. Yes, there are animals in heaven. Are our pets? I'm not sure, the Bible doesn't say.

Pets and Heaven

God is the one who made the animals. He wants us to care for them.

> Whoever kills an animal is to make restitution for it, life for life. (Leviticus 24:18)
> For every animal of the forest is Mine, the cattle on a thousand hills. I

know every bird of the mountains, and the creatures of the field are Mine. If I were hungry, I would not tell you, for the world and everything in it are Mine. (Psalms 50:10–12)

He provides the animals with their food, and the young ravens, what they cry for. He is not impressed by the strength of a horse; He does not value the power of a man. The Lord values those who fear Him, those who put their hope in His faithful love. (Psalms 147:9–11)

Day 15

Illegal Entry

I was up early one morning doing dishes. I had my back to the front door. One of the boys from down the street came over. I guess he noticed me in the kitchen. He thought it would be funny to sneak in on me and goose me. I was very angry with him. Not because he goosed me. Because he just walked in the house uninvited. He didn't knock, and no one knew he was coming. Years later, a biblical truth came from this incident. It is wrong for someone to walk in your house uninvited. Just as it is wrong for us as humans to just walk in someone's house, Jesus will not just walk into our hearts. He died for a chance that you might accept Him. He bled for all mankind. He will not break the door down. He will not sneak into your heart. He will not enter without permission.

> Listen! I stand at the door and knock. If anyone hears My voice and opens the door, I will come in to him and have dinner with him, and he with Me. (Revelation 3:20)

Jesus Will Stand

This passage says *anyone*, Jesus gives all mankind a choice. He will not force us to be with Him in heaven. He also extends the invitation to everyone ever born.

Jesus said, "I *stand* at the door." He did not say, "You have no choice." He also said, "If *anyone* hears and opens." He did not say, "Only certain people will be able to have me."

I was once told that there has been ten messiahs. Any messiahs that were not Jesus are fake and liars from hell.

> So Jesus said again, "I assure you: I am the door of the sheep. All who came before Me are thieves and robbers, but the sheep didn't listen to them. I am the door. If ANYONE enters by Me, he will be saved and will come in and go out and find pasture. (John 10:7)
>
> A thief comes only to steal and to kill and destroy. I have come so that they may have life and have it in abundance. (Leviticus 24:18)

Day 16

Adult Deception

There was a sandpit in the backyard. I spent a lot of time there. On one such day, I was playing in it. My sisters said to me, "Hey, let's go in the woods." I liked playing in the woods, so I went. We walked all the way to the landlord's house. I didn't know we were going to do this. When we got there, his daughter and her friend who were older were standing with two horses, and he was there. There was a small single cab white truck in a field. He asked me and my sisters if we wanted to drive. They were like, "Yeah! Yeah!" So I went along with it. It seemed innocent. He got in the driver's seat and put one of us at a time in his lap. He would press the gas, and we would steer. I was last in his lap. This is when he molested me. I couldn't get away. When he was finished, his daughter and her friend took us home on their horses. This woke up a sexual desire in me that should not have been until I was older. It was this that the devil used to put me in bondage to the sexual sin of masturbation. I was nine years old. I found out later he was committing incest on his daughter. My bondage lasted almost forty years.

Sometimes We Are Tricked

In life, we may have times when we get tricked. We didn't see it coming, but there it is. So we are caught. In times where we find ourselves in that kind of situation, hopefully we know God. We can cry to God to help us get free. I did not know God. However, God has pulled out good from my bad.

> Everyone has to be on guard against his friend. Don't trust any brother, for every brother will certainly deceive and every friend spread slander. Each one betrays his friend; no one tells the truth. They have taught their tongues to speak lies; they wear themselves out doing wrong. You live in a world of deception. In their deception they refuse to know Me. This is the Lord's declaration. (Jeremiah 9:4–6)
>
> What then? Are we any better? Not at all! For we have previously charged that both Jews and Gentiles are all under sin, as it is written: There is no one righteous, not even one. There is no one who understands; there is no one who seeks God. All have turned away; all alike have become useless. There is no one who does what is good, not even one. Their throat is an open grave; they deceive with their tongues. Vipers' venom is under their lips. Their mouth is full of cursing and bitterness. Their feet are swift to shed blood; ruin and wretchedness are in their paths, and the path of peace they

have not known. There is no fear of God before their eyes. (Romans 3:9–18) And we have this command from Him: The one who loves God must also love his brother. (1 John 4:21)

Day 17

Sin Is Black

> What this guy did was very wrong. But let us look a little closer. He committed sin against me. What is *sin*? The Bible says these to name a few things: sexual immoral acts, lying, stealing, being a drunk, cheating, verbal abuse, idolatry, adultery, unforgiveness, envy, and the sort. So which one does the Bible say is worse? The sin you commit with sex because it is against your flesh. Okay, so which is the second worst one? None is worse after sexual immorality. All sin is black in God's eyes. He cannot allow it in heaven.

Trapped

As a young child, I am trapped in this sexual sin. To perform the act of masturbation, you need to think of someone. Well, I made up stories in my head. It didn't matter what guy I would think about. This action soul-ties you to another person. It is wrong to soul-tie whether you are single or married. The person you're soul-tying to is not your spouse. That is not good in the marriage bed. So to perform this act as a single person takes it to the marriage. You need to be able to stop doing this while you are single. That way, it will not go with you into your marriage. This is an act of sex. I did not understand any of this as a nine-year-old child.

This idea that I'm not so bad, all I did is tell a white lie. I guess that a black lie is worse?

> Don't be deceived: God is not mocked. For whatever a man sows he will also reap, because the one who sows to his flesh will reap corruption from the flesh, but the one who sows to the Spirit will reap eternal life from the Spirit. (Galatians 6:7–8)
>
> When Jesus stood up, He said to her, "Woman, where are they? Has no one condemned you? "No one, Lord," she answered. "Neither do I condemn you," said Jesus. "Go, and from now on *do not sin anymore*." (John 8:10–11, emphasis mine)

If Jesus says to no longer sin, then this means that there is a way to keep from committing habitual sin. If you pray this way, "I claim the blood of Jesus over my hands, my feet, my mind, my sexual organs, or my whole body. Please, Jesus, keep me from _____" (put in whatever sin that you are in bondage to), it is possible to stop sinning.

> Do you really think—anyone of you who judges those who do such things yet do *the same*—that you will escape God's judgment? (Romans 2:3, emphasis mine)
>
> But as it is, you boast in your arrogance. All such boasting is evil. (James 4:16)

More of God

It is the habitual sin. The people who when they know it is a sin and they make no effort to stop or change. God knows your heart. He knows if you are trying. Seek the Lord, and you will find Him.

> As a deer longs for streams of water, so I long for You, God. (Psalm 42:1)
> God, You are my God; I eagerly seek You. I thirst for You; my body faints for You in a land that is dry, desolate, and without water. (Psalm 63:1)

When have you wanted God this much? Are you truly seeking Him? How often do you talk to Him?

> But seek first the kingdom of God and His *righteousness*, and all these things will be provided for you. (Matthew 6:33, emphasis mine)

This says, "Seek the kingdom and His *righteousness*." This means stop sinning. Live right. How big is your God? My God made the world. I am now understanding so much more. I want more and more of God. I will never go back to the way I was.

Day 18

Alone at Times

We are going through life. There is a battle going on for our soul. Satan is hurting us and doing anything he can to keep us on the wide road. He has people who are under his control who do hurt us greatly. This causes all kinds of bad feelings and emotions. If we allow the actions of others to keep us angry, bitter, hating, fearful, and sad, then Satan can keep us from finding and choosing the narrow road. If we allow God to work in us, He can change and fix our hearts.

Left Alone

> I remember one day us kids went to a football game of our school team. At the end of the game, we were all standing around and getting together about to leave. I had to go to the bathroom. I told them this. I was not in there long. When I got out, they were not there. I looked for them. They had left me on purpose. This made me mad and sad that now I have to walk in the dark all the way home by myself. I started my walk to the house alone in the dark. I cut through a neighborhood so it would be faster. I did not see anyone anywhere. Then out of seemingly nowhere, a guy on a motorcycle came

up from behind me. He stopped and asked why I was out so late. I told him what had happened. He asked if I would let him take me home. I stared at him a little bit. I didn't see anything bad or feel anything bad. So I said sure. I got on the back, and we headed to my house. I directed him, and he said that is the way he was going also. He got to the end of our drive and asked me if I wanted him to take me all the way to the house. I said, "No, I can walk the rest." I thanked him, and he said, "You're welcome," and went back on his way. As I got closer to the house, I could hear my dad screaming at the others for leaving me alone. I was happy they were getting in trouble. My dad was getting his shoes on as I stepped in. You can imagine when I walked in the door he was shocked. I told him that a really nice guy gave me a ride home on his motorcycle. I think about this sometimes and wonder if that guy was just a guy God put in the right place, or if he was an angel God sent to answer a prayer of my dad's.

Alone in the Dark

There will be times in our lives when we have to go it alone. If we have Jesus, we are not alone. We may not have people around, but God will be there.

> Then the Lord said to Noah, "Enter the Ark, you and all your household, for I have seen that you alone are righteous before Me in this generation. (Genesis 7:1)
>
> I will both lie down and sleep in peace, for You alone, Lord, make me live in safety. (Psalms 4:8)

But each person should examine his own work, and then he will have a reason for boasting in himself alone, and not in respect to someone else. (Galatians 6:4)

In fact, all those who want to live a godly life in Christ Jesus will be persecuted. (2 Timothy 3:12)

Day 19

Looking for Church

> Our mom was not there to force us to go to church anymore. We started going to church on our own. I wasn't sure on which church to go to. The two older brothers refused to go anywhere, but the four of us younger kids started going to the first Baptist in town. A lady would come and get us. It was across a field from the Nazarene church. I don't remember when or why, but at some point, I started going to the Nazarene Church.

No Candy

> An older lady at the Nazarene church told me if I ever needed her to pick me up, she would. I thought it was strange for her to say that. She handed me her phone number. I said okay, and I took her number. I said, "It's okay. The lady who picks up the others also takes me." I guess she knew something I didn't. That night when we got home, she gave a candy bar to my brothers who don't go to church, and then as the others got out of her car, she handed them one. They all went in the house. Naturally I was waiting for a candy bar.

I asked, "Where is mine?" She said only those who go to the Baptist church get one. I said the two older brothers don't go anywhere.

She was like, "Oh well, you go to a different church."

I said, "Fine," and left. I may have been young, but I was not stupid. A candy bar is not going to make me decide to change which church I go to. I for one am too stubborn for that. As far as I cared, she could take that candy bar and…do whatever with it. I walked in the house; they asked me where my candy bar was. I said, "She wouldn't give me one." They said why. I told them, and they said the same thing. Those two didn't go anywhere. To which I replied, "I know, that is what I told her." I walked right to the phone and called that other lady. I told her I would need her to pick me up from then on. She asked what happened. I said, "I will tell you next Sunday." I did not ride with that other lady again.

Church Not at Fault

Someone from the Baptist church found out what she had done. They felt bad about it. That year on my birthday, they had a big party for me to apologize for the actions of that lady. I was very appreciative of the nice gesture. I always knew when people hurt you it is them, not a group. I knew it was not the church; it was that one person.

No to Bribes

You can't bribe someone to accept Jesus or to change churches. If they do take your bribe, then it is not in their heart or genuine.

> You must not take a bribe, for a bribe blinds the clear-sighted and corrupts the words of the righteous. (Exodus 23:8)
>
> The one who profits dishonestly troubles his household, but the one who hates bribes will live. (Proverbs 15:27)
>
> A wicked man secretly takes a bribe to subvert the course of justice. (Proverbs 17:23)
>
> A secret gift soothes anger, and a covert bribe, fierce rage. (Proverbs 21:14)
>
> Surely, the practice of extortion turns a wise person into a fool, and a bribe destroys the mind. (Ecclesiastes 7:7)

Day 20

No Bitterness

I guess the devil had a hard time getting me to get angry or stay angry. I just didn't and still don't hold on to things. I have a heart of forgiveness. He tried other ways to get rid of me. I was cleaning the vent in the bathroom. This is the intake to the central air. The dust is nasty. As I cleaned it, I cut my finger. The next day, it was already starting to swell. I went to school. It was a playday. It got worse. I didn't know how sick I was. In those days, the school had to get permission from the parents before they could take them to a doctor. My dad worked in the oil industry, and he was not in an office. There were no cell phones back then, so it took hours to get to him. They finally took me to the doctor. I had three red lines going up my arm. It almost got to my heart. It was blood poisoning. God protected me. This almost killed me. They gave me a shot and antibiotics. By the time I got home, I was already feeling better.

Children Can Accept

> I was at church when I first heard about following or accepting Jesus. I was ten. I went to the preacher after service and asked him what it meant. He said some nice things, patted my head, and sent me away. It was wrong for him to think that children can't accept Jesus. Just because we are young and poor that doesn't mean we can't think. All I thought was, *That was a waste of my time.* Later I was asking my sister about it. I said, "So if I die because he didn't answer my question, does that mean I will go to hell?"
>
> She said, "No, not if you don't understand." I think maybe I was closer to the right answer.

Truly Loving Jesus

Following Jesus is not about a church name. It is about loving Him. Talk to Jesus every day. What does that look like? It is when you get up in the morning and you can think, go to a place where you won't be bothered, and pray. Then before you go to bed pray. During the day read some of the Bible. It means spending time with Jesus.

True Heart

Children are not stupid just because they are small. Too many adults make the assumption that children can't think.

> As for you, Solomon my son, know the God of your father, and serve Him with a whole heart and a willing mind, for the Lord searches every heart and under-

stands the intention of every thought. If you seek Him, He will be found by you, but if you forsake Him, He will reject you forever. (1 Chronicles 28:9)

The intelligent person restrains his words, and one who keeps a cool head is a man of understanding. (Proverbs 17:27)

And you know that from childhood you have known the sacred scriptures, which are able to give wisdom for salvation through faith in Christ Jesus. All scripture is inspired by God and is profitable for teaching, for rebuking, for correcting, for training in righteousness, so that the man of God may be complete, equipped for every good work. (2 Timothy 3:15–17)

Day 21

Suffocating Experience

> My brothers thought it was funny to be mean. On night they picked me up and shoved me in Dad's canvas army bag. They laughed as I cried. I told them I couldn't breathe. They laughed more. I started to move the top of the bag up and down to get air through the hole at the top. When I stop crying and complaining, I guess they got bored of hurting me. They finally let me out. This kept me from wanting a close relationship with them. This hurt me deeply, and they barely even remember doing it. They think it was just harmless play, but it was not harmless to me.

Near Death

> One of my brothers got sick. He was sick for two weeks. Finally Dad took him to the hospital. He had an emergency surgery to remove his appendix. He was born with an extra layer of skin around it. That is the only reason he survived. This was very scary. He had this for two weeks before, and we didn't know. I asked him, "How do you know when you have an appendicitis?"

> He answered, "It is like no pain you have ever felt. It never stops hurting no matter what position you are in." This would prove to be very vital information for me later in my life as well as my brother surviving.

Not Being Close

Satan wants to keep us on the road bound for hell. If I had allowed anger against my brothers to stay in my heart, I might not have listened to one of them later. Many of the bad things even the ones we do, are used by Satan to keep us from getting to heaven.

> Your eye is the lamp of the body. When your eye is good, your whole body is also full of light. But when it is bad, your body is also full of darkness. Take care then, that the light in you is not darkness. If, therefore, your whole body is full of light, with no part of it in darkness, it will be entirely illuminated, as when a lamp shines its light on you. (Luke 11:34–36)
>
> Who is wise and has understanding among you? He should show his works by good conduct with wisdom's gentleness. But if you have bitter envy and selfish ambition in your heart, don't brag and deny the truth. Such wisdom does not come from above but is earthly, unspiritual, demonic. For where envy and selfish ambition exist, there is disorder and every kind of evil. But the wisdom from above is first pure, then peace-loving,

gentle, compliant, full of mercy and good fruits, without favoritism and hypocrisy. And the fruit of righteousness is sown in peace by those who cultivate peace. (James 3:13–18)

Day 22

Night Packing

> At the end of the school year, we moved again. This move however was different. I was already in bed. I got woke up and told to start packing. We packed a flatbed trailer all night long. In the morning, we moved the trailer to a location near my mom. Dad then took us straight to his mother and father in Oklahoma. He didn't get sleep until we got there. When I reflect on this now, after becoming an adult, I think he figured out and was protecting us girls from the landlord. I never got a chance to ask him. We spent the summer at Grandma and Grandpa's. Dad was finally able to transfer his job to Oklahoma. We then moved to a small town.

Sickness

> A few years later, our grandpa was in the hospital. He was not well. We all went to visit him. My father was color-blind. He only saw shades of gray. When he was at a stoplight, he would stare at the light to see when it changed. This day, it changed, and he went. Some young guys in a red convertible ran the red light. We hit them

> hard in the side of their car. My head hit the dashboard. This was before seat belt laws. I hit it so hard it moved my neck bones. I could see one protruding out after that. The guys were real sorry about what they had done. I think it really got to the driver when he saw how many of us were in the vehicle. The vehicle we were in wasn't damaged too bad. We went on to the hospital. We all saw Grandpa. He then died a few days later.

Family Relationships

Our father cared for us. I think he found something out. It is hard to be a single dad. In that move, I believe our father showed great love.

> If you then who are evil, know how to give good gifts to your children, how much more will your father in heaven give good things to those who ask Him! (Matthew 7:11)
>
> I am no longer in the world, but they are in the world, and I am coming to You. Holy Father, protect them by Your name that You have given Me, so that they may be one as We are one. (John 17:11)

DAY 23

Green Evil

My sister and I had both seen the animals in the window. One day, she asked me if I had ever seen the little witch-like green lady. I said no. She told me sometimes when she would look down the hallway at night, she would see this one-foot green ugly witch running toward her. I firmly believe we had demonic activity around us.

Demonic Attack

My brothers found some friends down the road. My brothers sometimes would spend the night with them. On one night, only one of my brothers spent the night there. He told me later that on that night, after everyone had gone to bed, he felt something choking him. So he quietly went into the bathroom. When he looked in the mirror, he could see a demon on his back. He physically fought this demon. He got it off him that night. This made him rethink many things. It was this that made him make his choice to follow Jesus. Both brothers moved out soon after.

Demons Are Real

I don't understand why people think that the *devil* is not after their soul. My brother is still alive, and he was directly attacked. People, we need to wake up. It is past time to learn spiritual warfare. If you don't wake up now, you will be deceived.

> On that day many will say to Me, "Lord, Lord, didn't we prophesy in Your name, drive out demons in Your name, and do many miracles in Your name?" Then I will announce to them, "I never knew you! Depart from Me, you lawbreakers!" (Matthew 7:22–23)
>
> Heal the sick, raise the dead, cleanse those with skin diseases, drive out demons. You have received free of charge; give free of charge. (Matthew 10:8)
>
> And they were driving out many demons, anointing many sick people with olive oil, and healing them. (Mark 6:13)
>
> "And these signs will accompany those who believe: In My name they will drive out demons; they will speak in new languages; they will pick up snakes; if they should drink anything deadly, it will never harm them; they will lay hands on the sick, and they will get well. (Mark 16:17–18)
>
> "What is your name?" Jesus asked him. "Legion," he said—because many demons had entered him. (Luke 8:30)

John responded, "Master, we saw someone driving out demons in Your name, and we tried to stop him because he does not follow us." "Don't stop him," Jesus told him, "because whoever is not against you is for you." (Luke 9:49–50)

Day 24

Choosing Life

Later in life when I was thirteen, my brother started witnessing to me. I thought that there was something like feeling a movement inside of you when you got saved. I didn't understand, and he wasn't sure how to explain. Then a few more years passed.

When I was fifteen, my brother asked me to go visit him. When I got there, the devil took an opportunity to try and avert God's plan. A friend of my brother from years ago when we were young in another state had reconnected with him. He came over to see me and just say hi. We started to enjoy each other. We hung out most of the two weeks I was there. The devil tried to use this relationship to keep me from God's plan. My brother was able to share a salvation tract with me. This tract finally answered my question. You just choose to believe. When you make a decision to trust and follow Jesus, it is just that a decision. I thought about it the remaining time I was there. On the trip back home, I decided to follow Jesus. When I arrived home, I went straight to my bedroom, closed the door, knelt beside my bed, and accepted Jesus. I didn't go to church. I didn't talk to a preacher. I didn't feel some weird feeling. There is no

> name above me except Jesus Christ. I'm not part of some organization. I choose to follow Him. No one talked to me to push me into the choice. I made the choice. Becoming a Christian is not about the name or religion of the church you go to. It is all about following Jesus. It is a point in time. If I had died before I made the decision, I would be in hell. There is no such thing as evolving into a Christian. One minute you are not; the next after you confess out loud, then you are a Christian. Becoming a follower of Jesus is a conscious choice, not a slow work in your mind. It might take a few years to figure out, but the decision is a second. I stood up from my prayer and said, "Okay, God. I need and Bible and a church." At that time, we lived too far from any church.

Never Give Up

Never stop witnessing to those you love. Never stop praying for them to accept. Who knows where I would be now if my brother gave up.

> The one who pursues righteousness and faithful love will find life, righteousness, and honor. (Proverbs 21:21)
> For whoever wants to save his life will lose it, but whoever loses his life because of Me will find it. (Matthew 16:25)
> Then He said to them, "Go into all the world and preach the gospel to the whole creation. Whoever believes and is baptized will be saved, but whoever does not believe will be condemned. (Mark 16:15–16)

But honor the Messiah as Lord in your hearts. Always be ready to give a defense to anyone who asks you for a reason for the hope that is in you. However, do this with gentleness and respect, keeping your conscience clear, so that when you are accused, those who denounce your Christian life will be put to shame. (1 Peter 3:15–16)

Day 25

Decisions

I decided to travel on the narrow road. Once I made a decision to follow, I took the next exit off the wide road. Let's look at a family traveling through life. Let's say the dad is a Christian. The mom is not, and they have two children. Dad is on the narrow road. Mom is on the wide road. This is the one reason God says, "Do not be unevenly yoked."

> Do not be mismatched with unbelievers. For what partnership is there between righteousness and lawlessness? Or what fellowship does light have with darkness? (2 Corinthians 6:14)

Which parent do the kids follow? We all start on the wide road; they will naturally gravitate that way. We are born. Our parents put us in a car. We all have our own car. As children, we can't drive. So our parents tow us behind them. Regardless of which road they are on or how fast they are going, we are towed behind. At some point, we are freed from the tow and begin our own drive. We all start on the very wide road. If both parents were Christians, we might get on the narrow road early. If they are not, maybe later. The decision on which road is ours. We all have our own choice to make. God will not force anyone to live with Him. Jesus died for the chance that we would accept Him. He bled for all *mankind*. Just as it is wrong for us to walk into anyone's house uninvited, Jesus cannot and will not go against His word and invade our lives and hearts without permission.

> This is good, and it pleases God our Savior, who wants *everyone* to be saved and to come to the knowledge of the truth. (1 Timothy 2:3–4, emphasis mine)

When a person starts traveling down the wide road, it is smooth and easy. When you switch to the narrow road, it is rough with potholes and all kinds of road hazards. The wide, easy road may be smooth to be on, but it is rough on your emotions. The narrow road may be rough, but it is satisfying. When you marry, you need to marry someone on the same road. You are still in your own car, but you stop when they stop, and they stop when you stop.

Bible and Church

> My journey to follow Jesus began. I came to Jesus as we all do. I was a mess. The devil had, had a field day with my family. I was in bondage of sexual sin. I had no Bible and was not close enough to a church. My dad had been hurt by someone at a church and would not drive me to a church. I would have to walk. I did not know much about the Christian ways. Not long after I had told God I needed a Bible, our neighbor saw me outside and said God told him to give me a Bible. When he handed it to me, he was visibly nervous. He knew my father was resistant to church. He thought maybe he had heard wrong. I said, "Thank you. I told God I needed

> one." When I told him I had asked God for it, I saw him relax. Then we moved right next door to a church. I only had to walk around a fence. God is so faithful. I started to learn and have a heart for the lost. Satan will start to work overtime at getting either rid of us or to keep us from being effective in our walk with Jesus.

God Answers

When someone first becomes a Christian, they don't know how to pray. God knows this. He will honor your beginning request that are in line with His will. He will also do it quickly. This helps strengthen your faith.

> I sought the Lord, and He answered me and delivered me from all my fears. (Psalms 34:4)
> The Lord has heard my plea for help; the Lord accepts my prayer. (Psalms 6:9)
> All humanity will come to You, the One who hears prayer. (Psalms 65:2)
> I will give thanks to You because You have answered me and have become my salvation. (Psalms 118:21)
> On the day I called, You answered me; You increased strength within me. (Psalms 138:3)
> "Don't be afraid, Daniel," he said to me, "for from the first day that you purposed to understand and to humble yourself before your God, your prayers were heard. I have come because of your prayers. (Daniel 10:12)

But the angel said to him: Do not be afraid, Zechariah, because your prayer has been heard. Your wife Elizabeth will bear you a son, and you will name him John. (Luke 1:13)

There was a man in Caesarea named Cornelius, a centurion of what was called the Italian Regiment. He was a devout man and feared God along with his whole household. He did many charitable deeds for the Jewish people and always prayed to God. About three in the afternoon he distinctly saw in a vision an angel of God who came in and said to him, "Cornelius!" Looking intently at him, he became afraid and said, "What is it, lord?" The angel told him, "Your prayers and your acts of charity have come up as a memorial offering before God. (Acts 10:1–4)

Day 26

Life Happens

> My oldest brother came for a long visit. During this visit, he had something that he was charged with telling me. This should have never been given to him to carry. He told me that our mom asked him to tell me when I was old enough that my dad may not be my biological father. Our dad is part American Indian of the Choctaw. This was a real hard piece of information. It didn't take me long to decide that this didn't matter. I told Dad, "It doesn't matter. You're my dad." Mom later told me his name B. A. Khor. I always wondered why my dad would not call me by my name. My mother gave me the same initials as the guy she had been with.

Living with Emotional Pain

Children who are conceived have no defense and no control over who caused the conception. My father allowed my mother to name me. He lived with the constant reminder my whole life that I might not be his biological child. He showed me love just the same.

> For I am about to fall, and my pain is constantly with me. (Psalms 38:17)

But as for me—poor and in pain—let Your salvation protect me, God. (Psalms 69:29)

For if I cause you pain, then who will cheer me other than the one being hurt by me? (2 Corinthians 2:2)

Day 27

More Injuries

> I was in PE class. We did many different activities in this class. One was softball. I had my hands up to catch the ball. This guy that didn't like me thought that I would not be able to catch it. He ran from the other side of the field at full speed. Get this picture. He said he was trying to catch the ball; however, his back was turned against the ball. He put his arm across mine, and I was flipped on my back. He had his eyes on me, not the ball. After hitting my head many times and now being flipped on my back, I am in constant pain. I went to a doctor who said I had scoliosis. I cried on the way home. I had no way of paying for treatment of that. I would carry this with me for a while

Constant Physical Pain

I don't believe this doctor was intending on hurting me or that he was lying. His equipment was state of the art at the time. It was just inadequate to make an accurate diagnosis. I should have gotten a second opinion.

> But so you may know that the Son of Man has authority on earth to forgive

sins," He told the paralytic, "I tell you: get up, pick up your mat, and go home." Immediately he got up, picked up the mat, and went out in front of everyone. As a result, they were all astounded and gave glory to God, saying, "We have never seen anything like this!" (Mark 2:10–12)

Peter said to him, "Aeneas, Jesus Christ heals you. Get up and make your bed," and immediately he got up. So all who lived in Lydda and Sharon saw him and turned to the Lord. (Acts 9:34–35)

Day 28

Sex Education

> Public school has sex ed classes. The nurses are not allowed to talk about biblical principles. The nurse talked about when one should or shouldn't have sex. She said, "Not until you're eighteen." In my years in church, I never heard about waiting for marriage. That movement was later. My father never taught us about the Bible. Even though I had boyfriends, I did not have intercourse until I was eighteen. That boyfriend was not a good person. That relationship didn't last long thankfully. The next guy that I was with was nicer. He and I were only with each other for a short time. He is the one who actually said to me that the Bible says fornication is wrong. I looked it up.

For this is the will of God, even your sanctification, that ye should abstain from fornication (1 Thessalonians 4:3, KJV):

> I had never read this before. I looked in a dictionary for the words *abstain* and *fornication*. I didn't know what they meant. It means "keep away from sex before marriage." Now I know. If I do it again, it will certainly be held against me. Thankfully the next time I was to go to

> his house, I had got all the way to the walkway. Then I stopped, I turned around, and left. Jesus is more important. Now, that I am truly trying to follow, oh man, the guys showed up from everywhere.

> After this, Jesus found him in the temple complex and said to him, "See, you are well. Do not sin anymore, so that something worse doesn't happen to you."
> (John 5:14)

If Jesus told us to not sin anymore, then guess what He put in place the ability to keep away from sin. Claim the blood of Jesus over your life. Do this every time you pray and stop sinning.

> Instead, you act unjustly and cheat—and you do this to believers! Don't you know that the unrighteous will not inherit God's kingdom? Do not be deceived: No sexually immoral people, idolaters, adulterers, or anyone practicing homosexuality, no thieves, greedy people, drunkards, verbally abusive people, or swindlers will inherit God's kingdom. And some of you used to be like this. But you were washed, you were sanctified, you were justified in the name of the Lord Jesus Christ and by the Spirit of our God.
> (1 Corinthians 6:8–11)

Day 29

Getting Back on Track

I'm traveling down the bumpy road. Satan is trying his hardest with guy after guy to get me to go back. As I go, boulder after boulder are hitting my car, but now I am armed with the word of God. This frontal attack did not work. I had made a decision and took my stand. My dad told me once when I was younger, "If you believe something, then stand on it." Well, when I read it in the Bible, that was it. I was firm on the Bible being the God-breathed word. I thought, *I will never question the validity of the Bible! It is absolutely true.*

    I have been on this road just going from side to side. I still don't have very much knowledge of what the Bible says. However, at this point, I think I started to drive in a lane instead off on a shoulder. Just before I moved from this place, one more boulder came at me. This guy was trying to tempt me with the thought of wealth. Just stay with him, and he will surely take care of me. He gave me some sweet gifts. This I had to think on. He painted a real nice picture, but again God was top priority. After my graduation, I moved to college.

To Drink or Not to Drink

> At this time in my life, I don't know about opening doors in your life where it gives the devil rights to you. I said I was a mess when I became a Christian.
> I was still going to clubs and to others houses and drinking. I had only got what they call plastered one time. When I got up the next day, I was like, "That was not fun." All the movies make you think that it is so fun. It was not fun at all. I never did that again. But I was still drinking.
> I still at this point had not started to go to any church. I was with some friends drinking. I clearly felt an impression and heard the Holy Spirit say, "You don't need to drink anymore." I decided to quit. So far, for these few months in college, my sister had not been with me when I was somewhere drinking. Then we went together to her friend's house, and she offered me a drink. I said I had decided to quit. She said that I just didn't want to drink in front of her. I said, "Fine give me a beer." I drank half of the can. Then I said, "Okay, I drank in front of you. Now I am going to quit."

And don't get drunk with wine, which leads to reckless actions, but be filled by the Spirit (Ephesians 5:18):

This *verse* only says not to be a drunk. I was at that point not getting drunk. The Holy Spirit didn't demand I stop all drinking. It was only "you don't need it." I was just at a point where I was in agreement. I just didn't need alcohol anymore.

Woe to those who are heroes at drinking wine, who are fearless at mixing beer. (Isaiah 5:22)

When their drinking is over, they turn to promiscuity. Israel's leaders fervently love disgrace. (Hosea 4:18)

For if your brother is hurt by what you eat, you are no longer walking according to love. Do not destroy that one Christ died for by what you eat. Therefore, do not let your good be slandered, for the kingdom of God is not eating and drinking, but righteousness, peace, and joy in the Holy Spirit. Whoever serves Christ in this way is acceptable to God and approved by men. (Romans 14:15–18)

Day 30

Making Friends

> I made it a point to smile at everyone and say hi. I thought, *Well, I don't know anyone. This would be a good way to get to know people.*

God's Way

> When I got to college, my sister helped me get a job. I also started to go to a free karate class. I started seeing a guy from this class. He was an American Indian. It ended abruptly by him when I would not have sex. I was like, "Well, you don't care much about me. I'm doing this God's way."

Not Looking

> I told God I will not look for a guy. He would have to put one in front of me. Oh sure some guys came around, but I didn't feel like they were right. I then had gotten a second job in the cafeteria.

> This guy came through that worked a different shift. He introduced himself. I barely paid him any mind. Later I was walking, and another guy was going to the same place, so we walked there together. Then this guy I barely noticed showed up. We were formally introduced. Then we started running into each other around campus. I still wasn't paying him much mind.

Purpose

When you look for a mate out of purpose for God, it will more than likely last. If you're looking for a mate out of your own purpose or out of loneliness, you will have trouble making it work.

> God—His way is perfect; the word of the Lord is pure. He is a shield to all who take refuge in Him. (2 Samuel 22:31)
>
> God your way is holy. What god is great like God? (Psalms 77:13)
>
> Just as you don't know the path of the wind, or how bones develop in the womb of a pregnant woman, so you don't know the work of God who makes everything. (Ecclesiastes 11:5)

Day 31

Sickness

> Then one night as I walked to work, I got this pain in my side. It never stopped hurting. I remembered what my brother had told me. By the next morning, I realized it was appendicitis. When it was confirmed, my sister took me to the hospital. This guy was at the hospital with everyone who came to see me, which finally made me take notice.

Waiting One Full Year

> When I got out of the hospital and was back to going to classes, he asked me where I was going to church. I said I had not yet found a church. For a while, he got someone else to take me to where he was going. Then he started taking me.
>
> He asked me to his parents' house for Thanksgiving. When January came, he asked me to date him. In February, he asked me to marry him. In April, we made it official with a ring.

> I had some financial things come up. He said, "Let's go ahead and get married now. It will be better for you financially."
>
> I said, "No, God will take care of that. We have to date at least one full year." We set the date to marry on January 1.

God's Way

We are not here for us. Sometimes God allows us and may even direct us a certain way so that we can learn. All of us go through bad stuff. If we cling to God, that stuff will prove to be a teaching time. God can pull good things out of the bad. My intention when I married was pure. I can't say what my ex-husband's was.

> Therefore the Lord is waiting to show you mercy, and is rising up to show you compassion, for the Lord is a just God. All who wait patiently for Him are happy. (Isaiah 30:18)
>
> The Lord is good to those who wait for Him, to the person who seeks Him. It is good to wait quietly for deliverance from the Lord. (Lamentations 3:25–26)
>
> No one who waits for you will be disgraced; those who act treacherously without cause will be disgraced. Guide me in Your truth and teach me, for You are the God of my salvation; I wait for You all day long. May integrity and what is right watch over me, for I wait for You. (Psalms 25:3, 5)

We wait for Yahweh; He is our help and shield. (Psalms 33:20)

I am at rest in God alone; my salvation comes from Him. He alone is my rock and my salvation, my stronghold; I will never be shaken. (Psalms 62:1–2)

Day 32

God's Best Plan

In the summer, we went on mission trips. He went to one place. I went to a different location. I made a commitment to be there for the summer. One of my classes I had to mail back and forth to college. I didn't mind doing this. During my time through the summer on this mission, my back went out. I could not rise without help from my bed. I mentioned to them about the other doctor saying I had scoliosis. They sent me to get an Xray. He said, "Your back is as straight as an arrow." He did not know why I was in so much pain. The director said if I didn't get better, they were going to send me home. That night, I prayed. "God, I made a commitment to do this trip. I don't want to be sent home because of my back. Please heal me. If you don't heal it completely, then at least enough so I can stay for the rest of the time I am supposed to be here. In Jesus's name, amen." I started to go to sleep, and I felt my back getting warm. The next day, I was able to stand. God chose not to completely heal me. He just made it so I could stay for the remaining time. This was God's best plan for me. Then when the trips were over, everyone who went on any mission trip went to the church camp Glorieta. During this trip, we learned more about each other.

Dedicated to God

Let your yes be yes and your no be no. I said yes to this trip. God will honor our commitment to Him.

If anyone serves Me, he must follow Me. Where I am, there My servant also will be. If anyone serves Me, the Father will honor him. (John 12:26)

Because he is lovingly devoted to Me, I will deliver him; I will protect him because he knows My name. When he calls out to Me, I will answer him; I will be with him in trouble. I will rescue him and give him honor. (Psalms 91:14–15)

The wise will inherit honor, but He holds up fools to dishonor. (Proverbs 3:35)

So honor will come to you who believe, but for the unbelieving, The stone that the builders rejected—this One has become the cornerstone. (1 Peter 2:7)

Day 33

First Big Red Flag

On one night at camp, he said, "Well, we should go to bed." He took me to my room. I saw him go in his room. I thought he went to bed as I did. The next day as we were walking to the tabernacle, we passed some girls who commented on a game of spades. This game was played after I went to bed. I asked him, "Did you play with them last night?" He said yes. He acted like he was sleepy to get rid of me. I was in love, so I accepted his excuses.

I was also very naive. I believe people are telling the truth. I have no reason to lie. So I think other people are not lying.

Looked Right

I have to say, I felt like he was the guy God wanted me to be with when I looked at my list of what I want in a guy. Well, he had it, or so I thought. He is a Christian, licensed to preach, and seemed to be a happy person. In January of 1989, we got married. I did it! I waited and married a Christian in church. I turned around and got on track with God.

Sin Revealed

If I was praying to God every day in a prayer closet, going to a church that understood spiritual warfare and if I really understood being willing to give up all for Christ and also if at that time in my life I had understood how bad that sneaky kind of lying was showing his true character, I may be in a different place. I was too naive and too far from God to truly understand.

> God is not a man who lies, or a son of man who changes His mind. Does He speak and not act, or promise and not fulfill? (Numbers 23:19)
>
> You are of your father the Devil, and you want to carry out your father's desires. He was a murderer from the beginning and has not stood in the truth, because there is no truth in him. When he tells a lie, he speaks from his own nature, because he is a liar and the father of lairs. (John 8:44)
>
> Now this is the message we have heard from Him and declare to you: God is light, and there is absolutely no darkness in Him. If we say, "We have fellowship with Him," yet we walk in darkness, we are lying and are not practicing the truth. But if we walk in the light as Himself is in the light, we have fellowship with one another, and the blood of Jesus His Son cleanses us from all sin. If we say, "We have no sin," we are deceiving ourselves, and the truth is not in us.

If we confess our sins, He is faithful and righteous to forgive us our sins and to cleanse us from all unrighteousness. If we say, "We don't have any sin," we make Him a liar, and His word is not in us. (1 John 1:5–10)

The one who says, "I have come to know Him," yet doesn't keep His commands, is a liar, and the truth is not in him. (1 John 2:4)

Do not lie to one another, since you have put off the old self with its practices. (Colossians 3:9)

Day 34

Traveling Together

I am still traveling on the narrow road. Now my car is attached to another. We are riding side by side down the narrow road. Right? That is what I believed. If two people are trying to follow Jesus, they are going in the same direction. When one slows down, the other can say, "Come on, we need to go this way." But when you're on the road together, at least you keep moving—that is, keep growing as a Christian in Jesus. Right?

Truth Revealed

> On my wedding day, my father and I were talking at the kitchen table. My dad made a flippant comment that I was the biggest liar of the bunch. My brother was there. The one that talked the others into lying about me. I stuck my finger at my dad and said, "I never lied to you. It was always them lying about me. Ask him!" My brother after ten years finally told the truth. My relationship with my father got better after that. My father realized that I took all of those punishments without complaining because I knew that he didn't know. After having my own children, this was made even clearer to me. Sometimes you don't know whom to believe.

Undeserved Punishment

The times when we are punished for things we didn't do can make us very angry. We need to forgive those who hurt us. Know that by enduring, we will receive a reward. If you stay angry and keep unforgiveness, you will not get to heaven. You must forgive.

> So we must not get tired of doing good, for we will reap at the proper time if we don't give up. (Galatians 6:9)
>
> Up to the present hour we are both hungry and thirsty; we are poorly clothed, roughly treated, homeless; we labor, working with our own hands. When we are reviled, we bless; when we are persecuted, we endure it; when we are slandered, we respond graciously. Even now, we are like the world's garbage, like the dirt everyone scrapes off their sandals. (1 Corinthians 4:11-13)
>
> And who will harm you if you are deeply committed to what is good? But even if you should suffer for righteousness, you are blessed. Do not fear what they fear or be disturbed, but honor the Messiah as Lord in your hearts. Always be ready to give a defense to anyone who asks you for a reason for the hope that it is you. However, do this with gentleness and respect, keeping your conscience clear, so that when you are accused, those who denounce your Christian life will be put to shame. For it is better to suffer for

doing good, if that should be God's will, than for doing evil. For Christ also suffered for sins once for all, the righteous for the unrighteous, that He might bring you to God, after being put to death in the fleshly realm but made alive in the spiritual realm. (1 Peter 3:13–18)

Day 35

Need to Express

> I talk a lot. I give details about things. I do this, and I have recently found out that the Holy Spirit gives me information as I am talking.
>
> Well, I had just had our first son in November 1990. He wasn't even six months old. I was telling my husband about my day, as I had done many times. At this time in my life, I did not yet understand about the Holy Spirit speaking through me when I talk things out with people. All of a sudden, my husband screams, "Shut! Up!" I was devastated. What did I do? He said, "I can't handle all of your talking." I was so hurt by this. It took a long time for me to heal from this one thing. He may have stopped many blessings from the Holy Spirit speaking to my spirit.

Letting the Past Go

> I started to go into a postpartum depression. My childhood was catching up. I talked with my husband about me going to a counselor, he told me I would be find and that I didn't need that. I wasn't allowed to go to a counselor.
>
> I got pregnant with child number two. I remember putting the first child in the crib and going to another room and just curling up in a ball and crying. I did this many times. I prayed a lot. My prayers were mostly lamentations. I started screaming a lot. I felt as if my husband barely tried to do, or attempt to do, anything I asked of him. I felt if he did anything, it was to get me to shut up. I continued to cry out to God. I couldn't understand why my husband, the licensed preacher, was acting this way.

Friend's Helping Hand

> A friend helped, and finally, I was allowed to go to counseling. I was still pregnant, so the counselor didn't give me medication. I told her even if I was not pregnant, I still would not take it. I need to talk out my problems. I did not need pills. She tried to get my husband in. I told her no way would he even want to. I was right. She said I should write down my thoughts so when I got to the counseling I would not have to try to remember. I went a step further. I wrote letters to my brothers and sisters. This helped me forgive and move past all the pain.

Difficult Times Alone

I finally got past the depression. I had child number two in June 1992. My first child was very difficult to raise. This was only made worse because I felt like I had no one to talk to.

Narcissism Allowed to Grow

I got pregnant with our third child. We moved back to Oklahoma right after he was born in December 1994. We also found out that my husband's mother had cancer. We stayed with them until we found a place to live. At some point, she told me something that at the time I really didn't understand. She said her son (my husband) had an "I" problem. I will have to say the full meaning of that statement didn't really hit me until we were split up many years later.

I felt as if he would press us down (me and the children) to elevate himself. If we ever almost won or did win a game against him, he would never play it again. Whenever he and I were having an argument about anything, I felt he always twisted what I said to make it mean something completely different. I felt like he also used to blame everyone but himself. Nothing was ever his fault. If I was not there to blame, he seemed to blame the kids or his boss.

God Will Answer

> My husband's mom died from her cancer. I really cared for my mother-in-law. She taught me things that my mother should have. She stepped in that role for me willingly. I saw her love for Jesus. It was very special. I wanted that level of Godliness. At some point during that year of her struggle to survive, I prayed to God, "I want a double portion of whatever she has, and I want to be on the front line of You bringing Your kingdom on this earth." At this point, I am still waiting for God's answer.

Kill Your Blessing

Don't stop others from getting healthy. When those around you are well, it helps you be better. If someone is laughing, others feel the joy of that laughter. If you stop those around you from getting better, that can have negative effects on you.

> Therefore, whatever you want others to do for you, do also the same for them—this is the law and the prophets. (Matthew 7:12)
>
> Do nothing out of rivalry or conceit, but in humility consider others as more important than yourselves. (Philippians 2:3)
>
> Just as you want others to do for you, do the same for them. (Luke 6:31)
>
> Each one helps the other, and says to another, "Take courage!" (Isaiah 41:6)

So you also have sorrow now. But I will see you again. Your hearts will rejoice, and no one will rob you of your joy. (John 16:22)

DAY 36

Wrong Answers

> At some point, I heard that masturbation was wrong, but there was no explanation on how to stop. My bondage had been going on for over twenty years. The problem with this sin is, I was thinking of other men when I would do this. I talked with my husband as much as he would. All he would say was, "It is your problem." Since I was doing this before we met, I thought, *Yes, I guess it is.* But that is wrong; it was not just my problem. Once we were married, it became our problem. When I heard it was a sin, I wanted to stop. As a woman, we are supposed to ask our husband. All he gave me as an answer was, "Well, if we both agree that it is okay, then it is fine." He was referring to the *verse* in 1 Corinthians.

A husband should fulfill his marital responsibility to his wife, and likewise a wife to her husband. A wife does not have the right over her own body, but her husband does. In the same way, a husband does not have the right over his own body, but his wife does. Do not deprive one another sexually—except when you agree for a time, to devote yourselves to prayer. Then come together again; otherwise, Satan may tempt you because of your lack of self-control. I say the following as a concession, not as a command. (1 Corinthians 7:3–6)

> This *verse* is talking about when you fast and or are praying for something deeply. We never fasted at all while we were married. I fasted for the first time in my life after my divorce. This *verse* is not talking about when your needs are not being met intimately. I still did not learn how to stop.

Intimate Growth

Men say, "I just don't understand women." *So*! You only need to study and learn about one—your wife. I needed my husband to hear me, to feel what I was trying to get across when I talked. I needed him to study me. You should never stop dating your spouse.

> About three different anniversaries, he would say, "Let's have twenty more years like this one."
> I was like, "No way!" I want us to get better. I don't want to stay like this.
> He would smile. "Awe…better yeah." I was like whatever, and I felt as usual, there was no change that I could see.
> On one occasion when we were having a heated discussion, we had been married for about twenty years. I said, "You still haven't changed at all."

> He proudly proclaimed, "Yep, I am the same guy you married."
> I said, "That is not a compliment." God asks us to leave anything that would compete with our relationship with Him. This is also true in marriage. If you don't nourish and cherish it, don't bother to pray.

> Husbands, in the same way, live with your wives with an understanding of their weaker nature yet showing them honor as coheirs of the grace of life, so that your prayers will not be hindered. (1 Peter 3:7)

I don't recall seeing my husband pray or have a quiet time ever, he may have, I just didn't see it. We only prayed together less than a handful of times. Looking back, I wonder if he wanted God's help.

Being Close to God

Closeness to God is essential for our life. We must continue in our prayers and reading the Bible if we want God to continue to guide us. The only way to renew our spirit is to let the Holy Spirit speak to us. This is how we know what to do and what the Bible means.

> Don't worry about anything, but In everything, through prayer and petition with thanksgiving, let your request be made known to God. (Philippians 4:6)
> Pray constantly. (1 Thessalonians 5:17)

If you remain in Me and My words remain in you, ask whatever you want and it will be done for you. (John 15:7)

In the same way the Spirit also joins to help in our weakness, because we do not know what to pray for as we should, but the Spirit Himself intercedes for us with unspoken groanings. (Romans 8:26)

He will pay attention to the prayer of the destitute and will not despise their prayer. (Psalms 102:17)

Day 37

Dead Woman Walking

On the road, we should be traveling together. I was sure God directed me to him. With that in mind, I will show you a road scenario. A married man and woman on the narrow road traveling; we start out at the same pace going the same direction, but at some point, the woman is like, "Hurry up. We are going too slow."

The guy says, "No, I don't' like this bumpy road. It is too hard to drive."

The woman says, "Just trust. It will be okay." But somewhere, he just pulled over and stopped. Well, the woman is attached to his car. She wants to keep going forward. For a while, she drags his car along, but this doesn't work very well. Eventually her car breaks down.

Empty without God

> There are five *love languages*: giving gifts, quality time, physical touch (nonsexual), words of affirmation, acts of service. My love tank was dry. I felt as if it did no good to plead with my husband for attention. I completely shut down toward him emotionally. I was dead inside. God asks us to leave anything that would compete with our

> relationship with Him. This is also true in marriage. If you don't nourish and cherish the relationship, it will die.

Spouses don't like it when they get whatever time is left over at the end of the day. God doesn't like your leftover time either. Spend time with God, not the world. This means stop watching so much TV. Stop listening to bad radio stations. Be on social media less. Read your Bible daily, even if it is just a few verses. Pray to God in the same place in the morning before you leave and at night when you are still awake, at least an hour before your bedtime. God doesn't want us to pray and then pass out asleep. He wants us to want Him. If you truly love God, Jesus Christ, and the Holy Spirit, then you will truly want to spend time with Him.

Longing

God wants us to want Him, to desire His presence over everything, to be willing to sell it all, if He asked us to. God told Abram, "Go to a place I will show you." So he starts a long journey. Why? Because he was close to God and trusted Him.

> I long and yearn for the courts of the Lord; my heart and flesh cry out for the living God. (Psalms 84:2)
>
> How I love your instruction! It is my meditation all day long. Your commands make me wiser than my enemies, for they are always with me. I have more insight than all my teachers because Your decrees are my meditation. I open my mouth and pant because I long for Your commands. (Psalms 119:97–99, 131)

Day 38

Your Belief Is Your Own

> My problem is I allowed my husband to dictate my walk with God. Ladies, your walk with God is yours. Do not let anyone stop you from studying the Bible or praying. Also, if your spouse is not teaching you, then you start looking for preachers who are preaching the truth and listen to them.

Prayer Works When You Do It

> One day, I was curious about what my husband brought to God in prayer. I asked him, "What do you pray about?" He said, kids, something was going on at work, some other things about church. I said, "Do you pray for me?"
>
> He said, "No, you're fine." I was to say, at the least, a little shocked. How can you say you love someone and never bring them before the God of the uni*verse* in prayer. Not only was he not praying for me, but he was not and I felt that he would not pray with me. I can count on one hand the times we sincerely knelt together and prayed. At this point in our relationship, I felt like I was a good maid and roll over.

Agape love—what is it? Giving oneself for the benefit of another even at your own expense. The man is called to be a reflection of Jesus to her, to give up for her. Women will respect, come underneath his lead when she sees him really honestly give up for her.

No Emotions

> I was dead emotionally and just going through the motions of life. I even had a hard time crying. I was always asking, "God, am I wrong?" I would also say, "This is not abundant life." One time I was talking with a friend and said, "Well, God says no man put a marriage asunder. I guess this is my lot in life, and I am just stuck with him."
>
> I prayed for years our marriage would get better. I tried to get him to go to marriage counseling or just one of those marriage conferences. He wouldn't even think about it. You can only change yourself. I was in fact at a place where the enemy could attack.

You Follow God

Your Christian walk is yours and yours alone. No one will answer for your walk but you. Do not let someone else keep you from praying or reading the Bible. God desires our time. He wants each of us to stop during the day and talk to Him.

> So Peter turned around and saw the disciple Jesus loved following them. That disciple was the one who leaned back against Jesus at the supper and asked,

"Lord, who is the one that's going to betray You?" When Peter saw him, he said to Jesus, "Lord—what about him?" "If I want him to remain until I come," Jesus answered, "what is that to you? As for you, follow Me." So this report spread to the brothers that this disciple would not die. Yet Jesus did not tell him that he would not die, but, "If I want him to remain until I come, what is that to you?" This is the disciple who testifies to these things and who wrote them down. We know that his testimony is true. And there are also many other things that Jesus did, which, if they were written one by one, I suppose not even the world itself could contain the books that would be written. (John 21:20–25)

But the message is very near you, in your mouth and in your heart, so that you may follow it. See today I have set before you life and prosperity, death and adversity. For I am commanding you today to love the Lord your God, to walk in His ways, and to keep His commands, statutes, and ordinances, so that you may live and multiply, and the Lord your God may bless you in the land you are entering to possess. (Deuteronomy 30:14–16)

For you were called to this, because Christ also suffered for you, leaving you an example, so that you should follow in His steps. (1 Peter 2:21)

Don't turn away to follow worthless things that can't profit or deliver you; they are worthless. (1 Samuel 12:21)

"Follow Me," Jesus told them, "and I will make you fish for, people!" (Mark 1:17)

Day 39

Walking Away

The cars are broken down on the narrow road. The cars are towed to a repair shop. However, the repairmen are not allowed to do any work on his car. She is trying to get repairs on her car, but they can't get her car back on the road without his getting repaired. His car started to run, and so we left the repair shop. The problem was that he took us back to the wide road, but isn't it, "Once saved always saved." No, I am sorry to have to break your theology.

> They have gone astray by abandoning the straight path and have followed the path of Balaam, the son of Bosor, who loved the wages of unrighteousness. (2 Peter 2:15)
>
> And these are the ones sown on rocky ground: when they hear the word, immediately they *receive* it with joy. But they have no root in themselves; they are short-lived. When pressure or persecution comes because of the word, they immediately stumble. (Mark 4:16–17, my emphasis)
>
> For the love of money is a root of all kinds of evil, and by craving it, some

have wandered away from the faith and pierced themselves with many pains. (1 Timothy 6:10)

There are many more.

Yes, you can give up your salvation by turning back, going back to your sin nature. God will never leave us, but we can leave Him. God will not force you to love Him.

Leaving God

If you walk away from God, He will not force you to stay. God cannot allow sin in heaven. If you choose to live in habitual sin, you cannot live with God. If you will not forgive, you cannot live with God. God loves us so much and wants us to be free. But we have to love God also.

> Timothy, guard what has been entrusted to you, avoiding irreverent, empty speech and contradictions from the "knowledge" that falsely bears that name. By professing it, some people have deviated from the faith. Grace be with all of you. (1 Timothy 6:20–21)
> Now the Spirit explicitly says that in later times some will depart from the faith, paying attention to deceitful spirits and the teachings of demons. (1 Timothy 4:1)
> They have deviated from the truth, saying that the resurrection has already taken place, and are overturning the faith of some. (2 Timothy 2:18)
> For it would have been better for them not to have known the way of righ-

teousness than, after knowing it, to turn back from the holy command delivered to them. (2 Peter 2:21)

My brothers, if any amoung you strays from the truth, and someone turns him back. (James 5:19)

Remember then how far you have fallen; repent, and do the works you did at first. Otherwise, I will come to you and remove your lampstand from its place—unless you repent. (Revelation 2:5)

Day 40

Message of Death

Satan will send people to speak death into your life. Do not allow people to give you a message, especially people you do not know. If you don't know for sure if they are Christians, tell them, "No, you need to leave." Then you walk away. I was somewhere I could not even tell you where. This guy I did not know from a hole in the ground walked right up to me and started talking about how he could read palms. I resisted at first, but he went on and on. I finally gave in. I should have told him to get lost. Instead I stuck my hand out. He immediately said I would go through a terrible divorce. He said other stuff, but that didn't matter. He accomplished his goal. Even though I didn't go seek this guy out, I didn't give him money, I still opened a door to Satan, and death was spoken over my marriage. No, my marriage was not a very good one, but people can change. However, you can only change yourself. Never let people you don't know give you a message.

More Deception

> Later I worked for a lady. She was a *realtor*. When we started the process of buying a house, my husband said, "Let's have her help us." Then at one point, he got really angry about losing a piece of property. He wrote a terrible scathing e-mail to her. The problem is he did it on my e-mail address. This made her at first think that I had written it. She knew me better than that.
>
> It was such a terrible letter that she said to me later, "Don't let this cause you to divorce."
>
> I told her, "That wouldn't get me to leave."

Inviting in the Enemy

> Satan had been trying to destroy our marriage for years. Satan wants to destroy every marriage. I was trying to hold on, because of my belief in God's word. My inner commitment to my husband however was dead.
>
> I was trying to get my husband to pay some attention to me. He told me that I required so much attention that he would not have enough time to do work so that the bills were paid.
>
> My husband knew this guy before we met. I will call him Mr. B. Mr. B had been living out of the country. When he got back, he had nowhere to go. My husband said we should help. Mr. B move into our garage, but then my husband charged him rent.

> But now I am writing you not to associate with anyone who *claims* to be a believer who is sexually immoral or

greedy, an idolater or verbally abusive, a drunkard or a swindler. Do not even eat with such a person. (1 Corinthians 5:11, my emphasis)

Speak Life

Encourage people. Let them know you care. You have to open your mouth. Speak words that build others up: "You look good today," Have a great week," "Can I pray for you?" Most people are in a bit of discouragement. So your kind word will go a long way.

> The mouth of the righteous is a fountain of life, but the mouth of the wicked conceals violence. (Proverbs 10:11)
> My mouth speaks wisdom; my heart's meditation brings understanding. (Psalms 49:3)
> Don't let your mouth speak dishonestly, and don't let your lips talk deviously. (Proverbs 4:24)
> The tongue of the wise makes knowledge attractive, but the mouth of fools blurts out foolishness. (Proverbs 15:2)
> Life and death are in the power of the tongue, and those who love it will eat its fruit. (Proverbs 18:21)
> I know that His command is eternal life. So the things that I speak, I speak just as the Father has told Me. (John 12:50)
> So, too, though the tongue is a small part of the body, it boasts great things. Consider how large a forest a small fire

ignites. And the tongue is a fire. The tongue, a world of unrighteousness, is placed among the parts of our bodies. It pollutes the whole body, sets the course of life on fire, and is set on fire by hell. Every sea creature, reptile, bird, or animal is tamed by man, but no man can tame the tongue. It is a restless evil, full of deadly poison. We praise our Lord and Father with it, and we curse men who are made in God's likeness with it. Praising and cursing come out of the same mouth. My brothers, these things should not be this way. (James 3:5 –10)

Day 41

Battle in My Home

I thought, *Well, he is here. I should get to know something about him.* Mr. B and I told each other about our childhoods. Mine was bad, his was worse. This created sympathy in me. Then Mr. B started talking about his exploits. Over these months, I was spending too much of my time outside talking with him. Mr. B monopolized my time. This was real easy to do since I felt like my husband was spending very little time with me. Mr. B started complaining about his living condition, which I tried to make better. We did not have an apartment in the garage. We created a space. Make no mistake, we are led astray by our own lust. Unfortunately, this became true of me.

> But each person is tempted when he is drawn away and enticed by his own evil desires. (James 1:14)

Broken Down

After years of making up stories and sexual sin and put on top a bad marriage, it all finally resulted in me

> breaking down. It came out in physical action. This was the devil's side attack, because of frontal attack didn't work. Now I am kissing Mr. B.

Spirit World

> He started to tell me all sorts of wild things. He talked about astral projecting so he could see his grandchild in another country. He talked about portals where spirits can come and go. He said things like some people are keys to certain gates for the spirit world. I thought about these things. All of it was very strange to me.

Questioning All of Truth

> During this whole time, I was back and forth and very conflicted. I continued to beg God for truth. Then I felt like Mr. B started attacking my beliefs in God and the Bible. He said stuff like, the Bible is just written by men. There has been ten messiahs. At this point, I am questioning the validity of the Bible—something I never thought I would do.

Therefore, dear friends, since you know this in advance, be on your guard, so that you are not led away by the error of lawless people and fall from your own stability. (2 Peter 3:17)

Led Away by Deception

What do you long for the most? We are led away by desire, the desire in our heart. Satan will send a fake in our path to trick us and trip us. So we need to know what we desire and be on our guard.

> Don't be led astray by various kinds of strange teachings; for it is good for the heart to be established by grace and not by foods, since those involved in them have not benefited. (Hebrews 13:9)
>
> You have led your own selves astray because you are the ones who sent me to the Lord your God, saying, "Pray to the Lord our God on our behalf, and as for all that the Lord our God says, tell it to us, and we'll act accordingly." (Jeremiah 42:20)
>
> As obedient children, do not be conformed to the desires of your former ignorance. (1 Peter 1:14)
>
> You have no part or share in this matter, because your heart is not right before God. Therefore repent of this wickedness of yours, and pray to the Lord that the intent of your heart may be forgiven you. For I see you are poisoned by bitterness and bound by iniquity. (Acts 8:21–23)
>
> May He give you what your heart desires and fulfill your whole purpose. (Psalms 20:4)
>
> Take delight in the Lord, and He will give you your heart's desires. (Psalms 37:4)

Day 42

Get Egypt Out Completely

Thankfully God sees our hearts. He knows the lies that are around us.

I had stopped drinking and had said I wouldn't anymore to my husband. That was before we had been married. I actually had forgotten about that conversation. Through the years, every now and then we would pass the liquor. I would see the wine coolers and think, *That sure would taste good right now.* Egypt was still lingering in my heart. What does this mean exactly, you might ask. Well, let me explain. We all have stuff, sins that we are prone to. We have to leave that life completely. That life is Egypt. If we have Egypt in our heart, we haven't left it. Mine includes enjoying the taste of a good wine cooler to the point it makes me tipsy.

When things went very bad for my marriage, I went and bought some coolers. Satan will use anyone and anything around you to trip you up. He is roaring like a lion. Jesus is the lion of Judah and the Lamb that was slain. We are the sheep of the shepherd. Everything that Satan does is a fake copy.

Be *serious*! Be alert! Your adversary the Devil is prowling around like a roaring lion, looking for anyone he can devour. (1 Peter 5:8, my emphasis)

We All Have Junk

We all have a propensity to sin. Some are proud, some are homosexual, some are liars, some are angry, some are fornicators, some are narcissistic. We all have something in us. We all need to claim the blood of Jesus to keep from these sins. Satan will use all of our stuff to keep us off God's path and in bondage so that we will not fulfill God's intended plan.

Claim the Blood of Jesus

Finally I heard someone explain how to claim the blood of Jesus. You bow your head to pray. You speak the words, "I claim the blood of Jesus over my sexual organs. Lord Jesus, keep me from sinning against You. In Jesus's name, amen." That is it. The rest is up to the Lord. You can claim the blood on whatever part of you that is prone to sin against God. Sin no more.

Therefore, brothers, since we have boldness to enter the sanctuary through the blood of Jesus. (Hebrews 10:19)

But if we walk in the light as He Himself is in the light, we have fellowship with one another, and the blood of

Jesus His Son cleanses us from all sin. (1 John 1:7)

But now in Christ Jesus, you who were far away have been brought near by the blood of the Messiah. (Ephesians 2:13)

After this, Jesus found him in the temple complex and said to him, "See, you are well. Do not sin anymore, so that something worse doesn't happen to you." (John 5:14)

"No one, Lord," she answered. "Neither do I condemn you," said Jesus. "Go, and from now on do not sin anymore." (John 8:11)

DAY 43

Demonic Possession

> Deep down because I have the Holy Spirit, the Holy Spirit kept prodding me, saying, "That's wrong." There is only one messiah not ten. Even though the Bible was written by men; it is God-breathed. All the things that I was thinking and doing, many things were being said so much of it was wrong, but I couldn't see truth because of the cloud of lies around me. I had demons not just around me, but some were inside.
>
> Oh yes! Christians can have demons in them. Any part of your life that is not fully surrendered to Jesus can be controlled by a demon. You will have to either go to a deliverance meeting or do a self-deliverance prayer.

Conviction Is Good

> I was convicted of the things I was doing with Mr. B. I finally confessed to my husband, children, and my close friends. I quit for a time. However, I felt as if my husband didn't use this to repair our marriage. If I thought he had made any effort, we could have fixed it. I felt as if he just took the opportunity to use it against me.

Satan Almost Won

> I got depressed, and the hopeless feelings were overwhelming. Satan Almost Won. One night feeling completely unloved, I picked up a kitchen knife. I was going to cut my wrist. But God had other plans. I put the knife down. I just knew God had something for me. I went to bed. The next day, I told my husband, and I felt like he barely reacted. All the others were upset. I felt as if I was nothing more than a maid and roll over for my husband.

God Loves Us Too Much

> You may ask as others did, "Why did you stay so long?" God is the answer. Hope that my husband would change. Providence of God that at the time I couldn't see. If I had left too soon, I would have lost my children. I kept begging God to show me the truth. I decided I could not stay anymore in my marriage. I prayed to God, for Him to put it asunder. I said, "If You don't, I will have to." Less than two weeks from that prayer, something happened.

For All Have Sin

The Bible is very clear that no one but Jesus has no sin. We have *all* fallen short. We *all* deserve death in hell. But God put a plan in place for us. God has a purpose for every human life. Please if you are broken, as I was, call out to God. He will come through. Fall in love with God, Jesus Christ, and the Holy Spirit.

Jesus answered, "If anyone loves Me, he will keep My word. My Father will love him, and We will come to him and make Our home with him. (John 14:23)

Everyone who believes that Jesus is the Messiah has been born of God, and everyone who loves the Father also loves the one born of Him. (1 John 5:1)

Jesus Christ is the same yesterday, today, and forever. (Hebrews 13:8)

Therefore, no condemnation now exists for those in Christ Jesus. (Romans 8:1)

Now this is His command: that we believe in the name of His Son Jesus Christ, and love one another as He commanded us. (1 John 3:23)

Grace be with all who have undying love for our Lord Jesus Christ. (Ephesians 6:24)

Day 44

On July 4, 2016

Morning, seven o'clock. My husband stripped naked and wanted sex. I said no. I was going to have a really long day, and I did not want to. He tried to force me. Then when I told him, "You are not going to force me," he started throwing the stuff in the bedroom. He threw my things into the other bedroom. That is the last night we slept in the same bed.

When I got to my customer's house, I was telling them what happened. Then my husband called me and said he had signed me up for a conceal and carry class at the gun range. In this class, you have to fire a weapon, which would leave gunpowder on my hand. He said it would be on Saturday. I said, "What if I can't go?" To this, he got angry and snapped that I had until October. I found out this is when he most likely purchased the box of shotgun shells. It had five bullet shells in it. The bullet shells were the largest ball shells on the market. They will stop large animals. He meant to do harm.

On the tenth of July 2016, I was feeling bad; my stomach hurt. So I stayed home from church that morning. I told my husband I would work on laundry that morning, and I did. When he got home, he started to help but only so he could gripe about me going to eat with Mr. B the night before. My husband had gone and was gone almost all day. He never told me where he was. There was no food at the house. That Sunday, he said he had asked those at church about it. I didn't say much. Just that I didn't have anything to eat at the house. He left, and I finished what I was doing outside on the clothesline. He was inside cleaning the coffee table. He said, "I just want you to know that when I get done cleaning off this desk I'm going to blow my head off. Do you want to watch?"

I said, "No, not really." I had my phone in my pocket, and I took it out. I texted that statement to Mr. B. Then I sat down in a chair in the living room and started helping him clean off the coffee table. I was thinking, *Well, you don't have any shells because I had hid the ones we had.* At this time, I did not know he had purchased more. I put the trash in the can in the kitchen, then sat back in the chair. I found out he had bought more shells. When he came back in the living room, he had filled the sleeve with four of the shells, and he stopped and stood still in front of the TV. He loaded the last shell and snapped shut and cocked the gun.

He said, "I'm going to blow my head off. What are you going to do?"

I said, "I am going to call the police."

He said, "Give me your phone."

I said, "No." He calmly walked over to me and pointed the gun at me. The front of the barrel was about six inches from my chest; his finger was on the trigger. I was sitting in the chair; he was standing in front of me.

He said, "Give me your phone."

I said, "No."

He repeated, "Give me your phone."

I repeated, "No." His eyes changed. I thought he was going to pull the trigger.

He said very angrily, "Give me your phone."

I again said, "No." I was thinking, *This phone is my lifeline.* He grabbed my phone with his left hand and was still holding and pointing the gun at my chest. He jerked the phone back and forth so we fought for a bit. He sat the gun down; I am pretty sure in the chair beside me. My husband grabbed my phone with both of his hands after putting down the gun. He jerked so hard it gave me whiplash. I was being jerked almost out of the chair. I put my feet up on his chest to push him off, and he pushed down harder. He finally got my phone. He started walking to the bedroom.

He turned around and said with anger, "You f——g slut! Bitch!" I then stood up. He turned and went to the bedroom. I followed him, because I wanted my phone back. He had thrown my phone on the floor. He met me at the door and put his hands on my shoulders. His fingers dug hard in my skin so much it bruised me. He then shook me again so hard it gave me whiplash more. He said as he was shaking me, "Now you have a reason to divorce me."

I thought, *I already had one.* He stopped, and I started to try to get past him to get my phone. He kept hitting me with his open palms on my shoulders to keep me from my phone. This happened about six times. I then turned my back to him trying to get past him. He again with his palm hit me, this time so hard it knocked me to the floor. I saw the other phone on the coffee table,

> so I gave up on mine. I went and sat down on the couch and started trying to get the phone to light up. This way I could use the emergency feature. He came in and got the gun and went back to the bedroom. I was finally able to dial 911. The police came quickly. The cop knocked on the door with gun drawn. I unplugged the phone and went to the door. He motioned to me to leave. He checked the immediate area and put me in his police cruiser. After some communication and the police trying to call my husband out of the house by speaker and through calling my phone, he finally came to the door. He started to raise the gun like he was going to do a police-assisted suicide. He then put the gun down and had already thrown my phone beside the front door. He was taken to jail. He was in jail one month. A few days later when I changed the sheets on the bed where he was sleeping, he had hid four of the shotgun shells to keep the police from knowing he had, had all five of them. He plead guilty to all of this in a court of law. It is a matter of public record.

I had shared a *verse* with my husband on about six different occasions. He just ignored it.

> One who becomes stiff-necked, after many reprimands will be shattered instantly— beyond recovery. (Proverbs 29:1)

It is not about the sin we commit. It's about being too far away from God, Jesus Christ, and the Holy Spirit.

> Do not be conformed to this age, but be transformed by the renewing of your

mind, so that you may discern what is the good, pleasing, and perfect will of God. (Romans 12:2)

How are you going to renew your mind if you never put the good stuff in it? You need to be reading your Bible and praying.

Too Far Away

We can't expect God to do stuff for us if we do not have a relationship with Him.

> Be careful that you are not enticed to turn aside, worship, and bow down to other gods. (Deuteronomy 11:16)
>
> Be diligent to present yourself approved to God, a worker who doesn't need to be ashamed, correctly teaching the word of truth. But avoid irreverent, empty speech, for this will produce an even greater measure of godlessness. (2 Timothy 2:15–16)
>
> We used to have close fellowship; we walked with the crowd into the house of God. (Psalms 55:14)
>
> I call to God Most High, to God who fulfills His purpose for me. (Psalms 57:2)
>
> I follow close to You; Your right hand holds on to me. (Psalms 63:8)
>
> Thanks be to God for His indescribable gift. (2 Corinthians 9:15)

DAY 45

The Bondage Continued

> I was still in sexual bondage. Satan wanted me to stay there to keep me from God's purpose. I was still confused and being tricked. I felt like Mr. B. was trying to get me to where I would give in and choose to have sex. I was so broken. I prayed to God and said, "I have nothing left inside, no fight. If he comes at me, I will give in." I said, "If your word is true, then don't let it happen. No matter what." About a week later, God protected me in a special way. It never happened.
>
> I was still in the consequence of my actions when Mr. B got a girlfriend. I felt like he was no longer monopolizing my time. I started drawing close to God again. This time, there is no going back.

God Wants Us to Learn

He will leave us in our situation until we learn. We need to learn how to fight the enemy. The time is now. We are in the last days. God wants us to learn *spiritual warfare*. The *time is now*. Sickness is from Satan. Demons are real. Do not be deceived.

> Put on the full armor of God so that you
> can stand against the tactics of the devil.

For our battle is not against flesh and blood, but against the rulers, against the authorities, against the world powers of this darkness, against the spiritual forces of evil in the heavens. This is why you must take up the full armor of God, so that you may be able to resist in the evil day, and having prepared everything, to take your stand. Stand, therefore, with truth like a belt around your waist, righteousness like armor on your chest, and your feet sandaled with readiness for the gospel of peace. In every situation take the shield of faith, and with it you will be able to extinguish all the flaming arrows of the evil one. Take the helmet of salvation, and the sword of the Spirit, which is God's word. Pray at all times in the Spirit with every prayer and request, and stay alert in this with all perseverance and intercession for all the saints. (Ephesians 6:11–18)

But know this: Difficult times will come in the last days. (2 Timothy 3:1)

First, be aware of this: Scoffers will came in the last days to scoff, living according to their own desires. (2 Peter 3:3)

The one who rejects Me and doesn't accept My sayings has this as his judge: The word I have spoken will judge him on the last day. (John 12:48)

And to have authority to drive out demons. (Mark 3:15)

Then He sent them to proclaim the kingdom of God and to heal the sick. (Luke 9:2)

The prayer of faith will save the sick person, and the Lord will restore him to health; if he has committed sins, he will be forgiven. Therefore, confess your sins to one another, so that you may be healed. The urgent request of a righteous person is very powerful in its effect. (James 5:15–16)

He forgives all your sin; He heals all your diseases. (Psalms 103:3)

DAY 46

How God Works

My husband took us back to the wide road, but I didn't want to be on it. God broke my car free, and I sputtered into the repair shop on the narrow road. Soon I was driving on the road, but first, I was traveling real slow.

But God…

God's Protection through It All

This is a reflection of my life—how God works in even the bad things to bring about His plan, demonic attacks and all.

God has a plan for me. He also has a plan for you. If you follow Him and seek Him, He will use you for His kingdom.

> When I was born, I didn't get dropped on my head. This could have killed me. The time I saved the puppy, God didn't let me get hit by a vehicle. I didn't get addicted to cigarettes. After my mom left, I didn't go through abandonment feelings; this was a high protection on my emotions. When the guy tried to rape me, two ways I was protected: one I didn't understand what he was doing and two I bit him and got away. The

bike accident could have broken my neck. I do not hold bitterness against the guy who molested me. When my brothers and sisters left me at the football field, God kept me from being kidnapped or killed by a stranger.

I survived blood poisoning. My brother didn't die from appendicitis. He was able to tell me how you know you have it. He is also the one who witnessed to me later. God led my father to move us in the middle of the night to keep us safe from the landlord. When my head hit the dashboard, I didn't get a broken neck. My brother was able to fight off the demon and became a Christian. Then he started to witness to me. I became a Christian. God moved me right next to a church and had made sure I had a new Bible. I didn't commit suicide.

My back didn't get broken when I got hurt at school. I was shown the truth in the Bible about waiting for marriage to have sex, and I quit. I know I had appendicitis because my brother was able to tell me. During the mission trip, God healed my back only a little. Why? Why didn't God just take care of it all? I learned I was in sexual sin. I couldn't find the answer to stop. I didn't cut my wrist. I didn't get shot by my husband. After he went to jail, God protected me from having sex and got me out of the trap I was in.

God Has a Perfect Plan

We think sometimes the bad stuff we should not have gone through. Maybe God allows that to bring us closer to Him. God protected me. The bad stuff still happened. Where I am now in Jesus, I will stay with Him from now on.

Or to pay attention to myths and endless genealogies. These promote empty speculations rather than God's plan, which operates by faith. (1 Timothy 1:4)

Consider the work of God, for who can straighten out what He has made crooked? (Ecclesiastes 7:13)

For God has put it into their hearts to carry out His plan by having one purpose and to give their kingdom to the beast until God's words are accomplished. (Revelation 17:17)

Commit your activities to the Lord, and your plans will be achieved. (Proverbs 16:3)

The counsel of the Lord stands forever, the plans of His heart from generation to generation. (Psalms 33:11)

For I did not shrink back from declaring to you the whole plan of God. (Acts 20:27)

For I know the plans I have for you" this is the Lord's declaration—"plans for your welfare, not for disaster, to give you a future and a hope." (Jeremiah 29:11)

Day 47

Drawing Closer to God

I started praying more. Now my prayers are for learning and my personal life, my family, and my friends.

God was showing me how much He still loved me. I continued to draw closer to Him. I was at work one day. I was about to be done. I went to the restroom and realized I had a polyp. I have had one before and knew the signs. I had no time and not much money. I prayed, "Jesus, would You just take that out for me please. I just don't have time to mess with it. In Jesus's name, amen." I went on my way expecting it to come out the next day. When I said the word *amen*, I felt wetness and thought, *I'm bleeding from it. I'll take care of it when I get home.* I got home and went to the bathroom, and it was there. I thought, *Wow! That was fast. Thank you, Jesus.* God healed me to show me He still loved me.

Feeling God Again

I have had multiple injuries to my back and neck. A friend told me about her chiropractor. I started to go to him for treatment. I had been going to a friend's house for church after my husband went to jail. One day, I was at the chiropractic office. I picked up a book from his church (Church Eleven 32) that he had brought to his office. The book is called *Stories*. If God had healed my back when I was on the mission trip, I would never have been at this office to get that book. I read this book and felt the Holy Spirit pull me to go to that church. It was such a strong pull. I have never felt anything like that before. The following Sunday, I was at Church Eleven 32. I am now a member.

One Sunday, it was raining real bad. As I usually do, I got up and dressed to go to church. I walked in the living room and felt like something was in my way and not letting me leave the house. I have never felt anything like this before. I was like, "It is Sunday. We go to church on Sunday." I was being totally blocked from leaving the house. I said, "Okay, fine, I will stay." I turned on the music and praised God at home. I figured maybe God didn't let me leave because I would wreck my car in the rain.

A few days later, I watched the sermon online. On YouTube, they post other videos that you might be interested in. I saw something with a family I recognized from a book I had read a year before. The book was *Heaven Is For Real*. When the sermon was done, I clicked on the other program. It was *Sid Roth It's Supernatural*. The third one to play was the testimony of an ex-Satanist. He had served Satan for twenty-five years. I was intrigued by his salvation experience.

I started watching his preaching and many other videos on YouTube. I started to learn so fast. I could barely keep up with myself. All the stuff I should have

> known years before, I was learning in a few short months. I was also learning about the strange things that Mr. B had talked about, like you have to have demons take your soul when you astral-project. I also started learning about how to command the demons to get out of me and away from me.

God Loves Us

When we draw near to God, He will draw near to us. God does love everyone. He wants our fellowship. God speaks to us through the Holy Spirit. If I had not been injured so much, I would not have needed the chiropractic care and would not have been led to that church and so on.

> I speak the truth in Christ—I am not lying; my conscience is testifying to me with the Holy Spirit. (Romans 9:1)
> When they had prayed, the place where they were assembled was shaken, and they were all filled with the Holy Spirit and began to speak God's message with boldness. (Acts 4:31)
> Therefore I am informing you that no one speaking by the Spirit of God says, "Jesus is cursed," and no one can say, "Jesus is Lord," except by the Holy Spirit. (1 Corinthians 12:3)
> When the Spirit of truth comes, He will guide you into all the truth. For He will not speak on His own, but He will speak whatever He hears. He will

also declare to you what is to come. (John 16:13)

If I drive out demons by the Spirit of God, then the kingdom of God has come to you. (Matthew 12:28)

So when they arrest you and hand you over, don't worry beforehand what you will say. On the contrary, whatever is given to you in that hour—say it. For it isn't you speaking, but the Holy Spirit. (Mark 13:11)

DAY 48

Learning the Power of Jesus

> One particular day, I was driving. Out of the blue, I started crying. I thought about what was going on in my life at the time. Everything was going really good. There was no reason for me to be sad. As I thought on this, it occurred to me that I must have a depression demon in me. I said, "I command you now to leave me. Get out! Leave now in Jesus's name." I literally felt it leave my body and go out of the car. I was instantly happy. A few days later, I felt it trying to come back. I said, "No, I already told you to leave. I command you to leave in Jesus's name." I felt it leave again. I started to pray this way every day. "I command any demons that are in me, on me, in this room, in this house, in this neighborhood to leave now in Jesus's name. Go where Jesus is sending you and never return. In Jesus's name, amen."

Satan Lies, Lies, Lies

> Why do people hate God? Satan is a liar. God, Jesus Christ, and The Holy Spirit are truth. In hell, there

> will only be torment, burning, and utter aloneness. In heaven, there is peace, fellowship, and love.
>
> Satan lies to everyone; he lies to all. What makes you think he would actually tell you the truth? Satan will attack those who are a danger to him. God is concerned with our heart. Satan hurts you and then frames God for it. The demonic world is real. You can put your head in the sand if you want, but you will not be ready when the attack comes.
>
> I was learning about the courts of heaven, generational and bloodline curses, you can find all of these on YouTube, also about commanding demons to leave and claiming the blood of Jesus over your life. Finally I learned if you pray, "I claim the blood of Jesus over my sexual organs," then you can have true freedom. I was finally free from the sexual bondage. Now I claim the blood of Jesus over my whole body.

Hearing Truth Again

The *power* is in the name of *Jesus*. We command the demons in Jesus's name. They have no choice but to listen. Torment and utter aloneness is all that is waiting for those without Jesus. True freedom, peace, and good life are only through Jesus. I did not say easy, I said good.

> You are of your father the devil, and you want to carry out your father's desires. He was a murderer from the beginning and has not stood in the truth, because there is no truth in him. When he tells a lie, he speaks from his own nature, because he is a liar and the father of liars. (John 8:44)

To open their eyes so they may turn from darkness to light and from the power of Satan to God, that by faith in Me they may receive forgiveness of sins and a share among those who are sanctified. (Acts 26:18)

The coming of the lawless one is based on Satan's working, with all kinds of false miracles, signs, and wonders. and with every unrighteous deception among those who are perishing. They perish because they did not accept the love of the truth in order to be saved. (1 Thessalonians 2:9–10)

Keeping our eyes on Jesus, the source and perfecter of our faith, who for the joy that lay before Him endured a cross and despised the shame and has sat down at the right hand of God's throne. (Hebrews 12:2)

So the great dragon was thrown out—the ancient serpent, who is called the Devil and Satan, the one who deceives the whole world. He was thrown to earth, and his angels with him. (Revelation 12:9)

A truthful witness rescues lives, but one who utters lies is deceitful. (Proverbs 14:25)

A false witness will not go unpunished, and one who utters lies will not escape. (Proverbs 19:5)

Day 49

Visible Change

> I went to church, and a lady who had not seen me for a while looked at me. She said, "You look lighter."
>
> I looked at her and said, "I am much lighter. God is good."

Choose Love

God loves us. Jesus Christ loves us. The Holy Spirit loves us. God wants us to want to spend time with Him. You're filling your head with all of these things that don't matter and neglecting the *one* thing that does matter *most*.

I have been through a lot of stuff. My mom was with another man. Well I got a DNA test. The other man is my biological father. My dad who raised me is part American Indian. I have no Indian blood. Things like this give people excuses to remain bitter. Nobody benefits from bitterness. That is not what God wants us to do.

> All bitterness, anger and wrath, shouting and slander must be removed from you, along with all malice. And be kind and compassionate to one another, forgiving

one another, just as God also forgave you in Christ. (Ephesians 4:31–32)

Jesus wants *everyone* to accept Him.

> For God loved the world in this way: He gave His One and Only Son, so that *everyone* who believes in Him will not perish but have eternal life (John 3:16, emphasis mine).

It doesn't say only certain people. Those who have truly become Christians are the bride of Christ. He will come and get His bride. If there is anything that I have put in this book that you are not sure of, then pray to God that He will show you.

No Fear

Remember you don't need to have or live in fear. If you are following close to God, Jesus Christ and the Holy Spirit, then through Jesus, you command the demons.

> Now if any of you lacks wisdom, he should ask God, who gives to all generously and without criticizing, and it will be given to him. (James 1:5)

Jesus wants us to *rely* on Him. It is *not* that Jesus won't give us more than we can handle, but it is we can handle it, because it is *through* Jesus.

> I am able to do all things *through Him* who strengthens me. (Philippians 4:13, emphasis mine)

What does this look like? Well, when you are hurting, whether it is physical or emotional, get on your knees and cry out to Jesus. When you are okay, get on your knees and *cry* out to Jesus. People, we need to realize; we are not here for us. We are here for God.

What does it profit you if you gain the world but lose your soul? Nothing! I have several nuggets of goodness for you to think over.

You can't put God in a box.

Don't let the word Christian keep you from Christ.

The Bible is a *love letter* to us from God.

Don't do things that will not aid you in going God's way.

When hope walks out, depression walks in.

Pride makes you fake, humility makes you real.

Read the Bible for yourself. The Holy Spirit will show you the understanding of His word.

Faith without works is a faith that doesn't work.

God will honor an honest attempt even if you are not sure on how to do something.

God is the only source for us; everything else is only a resource.

God is either everything or He is nothing.

The fear (reverence) of the Lord is the beginning of wisdom.

We can do nothing without God.

You can lead a horse to water, but you can't make it drink. You can lead a heart to *love*, but you can't make it fall. You can lead a life to Jesus, but you can't make them accept.

If you still are not sure if God, Jesus, or the Holy Spirit are real and love you, then ask God to show you. He will come through.

Satan wanted to keep me in bondage to that sin. He wanted to keep me from my purpose, but God had another plan.

We all have to live with the choices that we make.

Freedom

I'm not free because I got a divorce. I am free because of the blood of Jesus—His death on the cross and resurrection from the grave.

There I am putting along, then God showed up. He honored my effort. He didn't have to, but He loves us too much to leave us just barely going. He took my car and moved me to the fastest lane, put a rocket on it. I was learning so quickly, catching up if you will, on all things I should have already learned. When He got me far enough, He moved me back over to a steady-going lane.

Now I will never turn back. I'm sure Satan didn't want you to read this book so that you would also stay in bondage and not fulfill your purpose. But God has a better plan.

Changed from the Inside Out

God, Jesus Christ, and the Holy Spirit are in the business of transformation. They take a completely broken soul and recreate it into the most beautiful life. They give us a reason to be on this planet. Purpose, abundant life, is what we have when we accept the love that they offer us freely. No, it is not an easy road, but it is worth it.

> In fact, all those who want to live a godly life in Christ Jesus will be persecuted.
> (2 Timothy 3:12)

He has saved us and called us with a holy calling, not according to our works but according to His own purpose and grace, which was given to us in Christ Jesus before time began. (2 Timothy 1:9)

He will transform the body of our humble condition into the likeness of His glorious body, by the power that enables Him to subject everything to Himself. (Philippians 3:21)

And the peace of God, which surpasses every thought, will guard your hearts and minds in Christ Jesus. (Philippians 4:7)

Since by the one man's trespass, death reigned through that one man, how much more will those who receive the overflow of grace and the gift of righteousness reign in life through the one man, Jesus Christ. (Romans 5:17)

For in light of the fact that He died, He died to sin once for all; but in light of the fact that He lives, He lives to God. So, you too consider yourselves dead to sin but alive to God in Christ Jesus. (Romans 6:10–11)

Therefore, no condemnation now exists for those in Christ Jesus, because the Spirit's law of life in Christ Jesus has set you free from the law of sin and of death. (Romans 8:1–2)

And the smoke of their torment will go up forever and ever. There is no rest day or night for those who worship the beast and his image, or anyone who receives the mark of his name. This demands the perseverance of the saints, who keep God's commands and their faith in Jesus. (Revelation 14:11–12)

But these are written so that you may believe Jesus is the Messiah, the Son of God, and by believing you may have life in His name. (John 20:31)

So that in the coming ages He might display the immeasurable riches of His grace through His kindness to us in Christ Jesus. For you are saved by grace through faith, and this is not from yourselves; it is God's gift—not from works, so that no one can boast. For we are His creation, created in Christ Jesus for good works, which God prepared ahead of time so that we should walk in them. (Ephesians 2:7–10)

Keep yourselves in the love of God, expecting the mercy of our Lord Jesus Christ for eternal life. (Jude 1:21)

Jesus Christ is the same yesterday, today, and forever. (Hebrews 13:8)

Nothing profane will ever enter it: no one who does what is vile or false, but only those written in the Lamb's book of life. (Revelation 21:27)

Those who practice habitual sin, will not enter the gates of heaven.

Day 50

If you have never given your life to Jesus Christ, and you want to...

Pray This Prayer

> Lord Jesus, I know I am a sinner. Please *forgive me* of my sins. I forgive those who have hurt me. I want you to be Lord of my life. I believe you came, were born to a virgin, died on the cross for me, and rose from the grave.
> Thank you for saving me.
> In Jesus's name, amen.

You may say, "I can't forgive that person. They hurt me so bad. We have all done bad things to others."

Not forgiving is like you drinking poison and expecting the other person to die. Or you may say, "I don't want them to get away with what they did to me." Forgiving them is not letting them off the hook. It is taking them off your hook and putting them on Jesus's hook. If you want Jesus to forgive you, then you need to forgive others.

Jesus is the *only* way.

> For if you forgive people their wrongdoing, your heavenly Father will forgive you as well. But if you don't forgive people,

your Father will not forgive your wrongdoing. (Mathew 6:14–15)

So My heavenly Father will also do to you if each of you does not forgive his brother from his heart. (Mathew 18:35)

It is better to take refuge in the Lord than to trust in man. (Psalms 118:8)

About the Author

Brenda Knox has lived a life of moving from place to place. She is the youngest of six children. She has had to live through many hurts; however, she has overcome them. As a child, she was deeply hurt by a man she did not know. This caused Brenda a great deal of pain for many years. After becoming a Christian at the age of fifteen, she began her long journey toward healing. Many mistakes were made along the way. At the age of twenty, Brenda married. She and her husband had three boys. Their oldest son is mentally challenged, so life as a mother was tough. The other two boys were compliant. Most of Brenda's energy was spent on her oldest son; although, she tried hard to pay attention to all three so no one was left out. When her youngest son was three years old, she began working as a cashier at a local grocery store. In her early thirties, she had a small vending business. It was short-lived due to chronic back pain. Later she started her own residential and commercial cleaning business. The business has been going strong for more than thirteen years. In 2017, Brenda and her husband of more than twenty-seven years divorced due to continual major communication issues. It was never her intention, but the marriage ended tragically. Brenda was very committed to her marriage. She took her vows seriously. Today, Brenda is moving forward in God's love and embracing the opportunities He is bringing her way. She is dedicated to her relationship with God, drawing closer to Him more with each passing day; it is with joy that Brenda looks forward to the next chapter of her life.

CPSIA information can be obtained
at www.ICGtesting.com
Printed in the USA
FFHW022029230719
53815915-59507FF

9 781645 150244